The Essence of the
GNOSTICS

The Essence of the GNOSTICS

BERNARD SIMON

Capella

This edition printed in 2004 for
Indigo Books
468 King St W,
Suite 500,
Toronto,
Ontario M5V 1L8

ISBN 1-84193-188-8

Printed in China

Contents

Introduction

Gnosticism is a system of belief that came to notice in the early years of the first century AD. While often operating from hidden places, it has survived in one form or another until the present day. Its adherents ranged from magicians to theologians, many of whom were branded as non-believers and heretics by the orthodox Christians.

The Greek language has two different words for knowledge: one of them represents scientific or reflective knowledge while the other, '*gnosis*', stands for 'knowing through observation or experience'. The group of people who became known as the Gnostics used this word to mean knowledge of a particular kind, which was not gained through intellectual discovery but through personal experience or association.

Such knowledge might be translated as 'insight', for *gnosis* involves an intuitive means of knowing oneself. By extension, knowing oneself is to know humankind and human destiny. Such insight involves a comprehension of spiritual truths which can both initiate one into the more esoteric mysteries and alert one to the awareness of the existence of the 'divine spark' within each of us.

The Greek word *gnosis* gives us both Gnosticism and agnosticism. However, agnosticism is the *absence* of the knowledge of the existence of God, while Gnosticism not only admits his existence but also claims to have special knowledge of him as well as spiritual matters.

According to the Gnostic teacher Theodotus, writing in Asia Minor (c.140–160), the gnostic:

> has come to understand who we were, and what we have become; where we were . . . whither we are hastening; from what we are being released; what birth is, and what is rebirth.

It is this 'special knowledge' of God which allows Gnosticism to be categorized as a mystery religion, although to be fair it probably did not properly achieve that status until after the birth and death of the man they called Jesus Christ.

When we explore the origins of gnosticism we find that part of its roots can be found in Zoroastrianism, the adherents of which believed in one God and were taught that the world was basically the battleground of two beings: Ahura Mazda, the god of light, creation, goodness and life and Ahriman, the god of darkness, destruction, corruption and death. This duality and conflict between good and evil or, rather, two polarities is an integral part of Gnosticism in its later forms.

Incidentally, a similar notion of duality and the juxtaposition of two polarities is to be found in almost every major ancient religious movement, both in the east and in the west. The other main influence on Gnosticism – the Dionysian cult and its later offshoot, Orpheanism – was based on a more ecstatic approach. In addition to considering Christian Gnosticism, it is sensible to look at these mystery religions and other such influences. Although all mystery religions, as a rule, have different features they tend to have certain points in common. These are:

- A ritual bath, cleansing or baptism, is part of an initiation ceremony
- Adherents to the belief take part in a ritual meal on a regular basis
- The birth and death of the instigator of the religion is in some way miraculous or remarkable
- At death, or on what appears to be death, he is restored to life but ultimately ends up in heaven thus proving his divinity
- There is often a goddess, or female principle, in attendance (usually a mother, but sometimes a consort)
- Whilst he is living, the divine man is ridiculed but takes care to impart certain arcane knowledge to his followers

By the time of Christ, Gnosticism was simply another embodiment of a very old belief system, therefore, going back at least to the sixth century BC and using what were perceived to be various types of 'magic' as its tools. We shall spend some time attempting to understand what gives Gnosticism its unique flavour and what eventually attracted people like Simon Magus, Valentinus, Marcion and other leaders to it. There were many sects within the religion itself and this diversity of belief, which we attempt to clarify for the reader, is an important aspect of Gnosticism.

In exploring the features of mystery religions in relation to Gnosticism we shall also discover that Gnostics differed from their orthodox counterparts in the questions they asked about what occurred before Creation. They speculated: 'If a creator god made this universe, then where did he live before that happened?'; 'Did he make our universe because he was forced to leave his old one for some reason?'; and 'Who created God, anyway?'

The originators of Gnosticism had their own supreme being, in one form or another, as well as a retinue of demigods and their representatives on earth. Their system of beliefs incorporated at least one 'exclusive' theory of creation, together with an account of the origin of good and evil. They later argued the need for an alternative to Jehovah (Jahweh), Judaism's 'jealous god', and at one point Gnosticism came very close to becoming the mainstream Christian church. It was not until the discovery, in 1945, of the lost documents of what has become known as the Nag Hammadi library – a collection of thirteen ancient codices containing over fifty texts – that we in the present day were able to have an enhanced understanding of Gnostic thought.

The scriptures from Nag Hammadi contain such texts as the Gospels of Thomas, of Philip and of Truth. A translation of the Gospel of Thomas into English demonstrates that Jesus seems to have taught his disciples in more depth than he did the masses, which is in keeping with the idea that there were three levels of awareness for Gnostics:

1. Those who had an inherent knowledge of the mysteries
2. Those who could be brought to an understanding of the mysteries
3. Those who would accept the teachings almost at face value

Later Gnostics believed that Jesus had taught the apostles sacred knowledge which was never put into writing, because its very nature dictated that it should never have been recorded. The disciples themselves were privy to these 'secret doctrines,' open only to the initiated, but only after the 'outer mysteries', or publicly-acknowledged teachings, had been mastered.

Some of the scriptures allow us to have a totally different view, unsullied by others interpretations, of the way in which Jesus imparted information. Here, the Gospel of Thomas speaks of the idea of an insightful life:

> And he said, 'Whoever finds the interpretation of these sayings will not experience death.'
>
> Jesus said, 'Let him who seeks continue seeking until he

> finds. When he finds, he will become troubled. When he becomes troubled, he will be astonished, and he will rule over the all.'
>
> Jesus said, 'If those who lead you say to you, "See, the kingdom is in the sky", then the birds of the sky will precede you. If they say to you, "It is in the sea", then the fish will precede you. Rather, the kingdom is inside of you, and it is outside of you. When you come to know yourselves, then you will become known, and you will realize that it is you who are the sons of the living father. But if you will not know yourselves, you dwell in poverty and it is you who are that poverty.'

There are several categories of information within the Nag Hammadi writings, but perhaps two of the most important are the liturgical and initiatory texts – those writings dealing primarily with the feminine aspect of God and the spiritual principle known as the Divine Sophia or Wisdom.

Exploring these categories we find that in the Gnostic creation myths it is Sophia, the last emanation of the transcendent God, who makes a mistake and creates the Demiurge – a vengeful, negative, egotistical creator God. She must then set about putting that mistake right, ultimately achieving union with the Christ figure in order to offer salvation and a way back to purity. In due course, Gnosticism developed a unique understanding of the feminine aspects within divinity and our exploration of such ideas begins to answer some of the questions which were posed earlier. The images, myths and symbolism of both the serpent and the labyrinth are potent gateways to understanding the feminine aspect of divinity.

We will consider those elements of gnosticism that are common to Graeco-Roman, and various other, pagan and occult religions. As we gain in understanding, it will be possible to compare the teachings of Gnosticism both with the Judeo-Christian religion and the later teachings of Paul, considered by some to have been Gnostic himself. We will find that Gnosticism was dismissed as heresy by Hippolytus, Irenaeus and others over the years – 'a species of infidelity in men who, having professed the faith of Christ, corrupt its dogmas' – and almost all genuine texts had disappeared by the sixth century. Researchers were left with very little information on which to base an assessment of the religion and it too seemed to disappear from view, although it had largely gone underground, being retained in organizations such as the Knights Templar and the Cathars. Where there was lack of understanding there was persecution and so coded information had to be left for others to decipher. Indeed, attempts are still being made to decode information on the Knights Templar and the Cathars to this day.

The symbolism of such belief, and the iconography which evolved, has given rise to much rich imagery which is still with us today and which has kept the spirit of Gnosticism alive. The idea of the Aeons, as they were called, as valid emanations of the transcendental god have relevance to our understanding of the first seven planets in the universe and the qualities that they are thought to impart to the human entity through astrology. C.G. Jung was able to use the personalizations of these qualities, as understood by the ancients, in developing his theories of the archetypes, thus helping us to understand the workings of the human mind in the present day. Conversely, the current findings of scholars, theologians and psychologists have given us a greater understanding of how and why the thinkers of antiquity built their theories of existence.

As the personalization and principle of feminine wisdom, Sophia herself is once again receiving the veneration she deserves as women worldwide continue to find their voices and understand their sexuality. As we shall see, even androgyny takes on a new meaning when looked at from a spiritual perspective. We find instances of Gnostic belief surfacing even in the modern-day world of pop music and media and, as time goes on, more and more people are beginning to appreciate the magical, spiritual and cosmic significance of this ancient system of thought.

The following chapters can do no more than scrape the surface of the complex subject that is Gnosticism, so in order to encourage the reader to continue his/her own investigations we include not just a bibliography of our own sources but also a list of further reading.

Chapter One:

Gnosticism Defined

In order to get to grips with Gnosticism as a system of belief it is important to define exactly what is meant by this term. As we saw in the introduction, *gnosis* comes from the Greek word meaning 'knowledge', but it is knowledge of a particular sort – that gained by personal experience. The term is usually used to indicate the awareness of the divine mysteries. The word gnosticism is a modern term, however, which has only been used to define the religion of gnosis in its own right since 1966, when a congress to determine its origins was held in Messina, Italy.

In order to help us define Gnosticism, one of the crispest definitions of Gnosis can be found in the 1997 edition of the *Cambridge Companion to the Bible* by Key, Meyers, Rogerson and Saldarini. They write:

> Gnosis . . . came to be used in the 2nd century AD to refer to a mode of religious thought that claimed to have exclusive information about the origin and destiny of the universe and its inhabitants. It taught that the material world was the work of evil powers, which had operated in defiance of the God of Light, who was the true and

> beneficent sovereign of the universe. Human beings were caught in material existence, and were therefore helpless to escape until the agony of divine knowledge came into the material world to explain and to demonstrate liberation. Some of the followers thought they could display their ability to rise above the material world by living in a strictly ascetic manner, while others took the route of unbridled self-indulgence as a way of showing that the material world was of no significance.

However, to understand gnosticism properly, and to find its true origins, we have to go back even further, to the time before the Christ figure.

One of the main things that separated the Gnostics from orthodox Christians was their mysticism – mystical communion with what was considered to be sacred. It began with their views of God and creation. Gnostics viewed the One – which they called the true or Unknown God – as also having a feminine part which was the Spirit. This duality was central to their creation myths and incorporates echoes of Taoism and the principle of Yin/Yang. Perhaps more importantly, this idea also has links with other religions of the pre-Christian period.

The *Catholic Encyclopaedia* defines Gnosticism as:

> A collective name for a large number of greatly-varying and pantheistic-idealistic sects which flourished from some time before the Christian Era down to the fifth century, and which, while borrowing the phraseology and some of the tenets of the chief religions of the day, and especially of Christianity, held matter to be a deterioration of spirit, and the whole universe a depravation of the Deity, and taught the ultimate end of all beings to be the overcoming of the

> grossness of matter and the return to the Parent-Spirit, which return they held to be inaugurated and facilitated by the appearance of some God-sent Saviour.

Gnostic myths state that the Unknown God is not the same as the Jehovah of the Jews, the creator god or Demiurge; that the world is a blunder caused by a fall from grace and a split in the deity; that spiritual man is related more closely to the deity than he realizes and is alien to the natural world, but that when he hears the words of revelation he becomes conscious of his deepest innermost Self – while he remains in ignorance he is lost.

Such ideas of self-realization were in existence well before the beginning of the Christian era. In the writings of Hermes Trismegistos (Thrice Great Hermes), thought by some to be the sayings of the Egyptian God Thoth, it is said that:

> He who knows himself, knows the All.

In another of his treatises called Poimandres, he states:

> Let spiritual man know himself, then he will know that he is immortal and that Eros is the origin of death, and he will know the All.

Coming right up to the present day, we can see that this main principle is put very succinctly by Keith Hopkins, Cambridge University Professor of Medieval History, in his 1999 book, *A World Full of Gods*.

> The core myth of Gnosticism turns on the belief that inside humans there is a spark of divinity, put there from a supreme divinity which is lodged in the high heavens of outer space. The divinity within each can be awakened by

> and discovered only through a process of contemplation and self-knowledge. This process of internal enlightenment or illumination can best be accomplished with the assistance of a divine mediator or redemption figure, who has a passing interest in the fate of God's creatures. A human instructor can also sometimes help, but even when Gnostics combine in groups, they seem anti-clerical ('bishops are dry canals'). Salvation is primarily the individual's own responsibility.

Later in the book, we shall look more carefully at the idea that each human being has the spark of divinity within himself/herself. We shall see that it is due to the actions of Sophia, the principle of Wisdom, sometimes known as the beloved – both of the wise man and of God. In *The Wisdom of Solomon*, written by an Alexandrian Jew in about 50 BC, it is said:

> Sophia is the breath of the power of God, pure emanation of the glory of the Almighty; hence nothing impure can find a way into her. She is a reflection of the eternal light, untarnished mirror of God's active power, image of his goodness. (Solomon 7: 25–26)

Divine Man

It is the strong sense of personal responsibility for, and relationship with, the divine spark which is marked in all followers of Gnostic thought and leads to the idea of the fully-developed Divine Man as a Redeemer. As far back as 593 BC, the prophet Ezekiel speaks of seeing the personified Glory of the Lord who would not abandon him whatever his trials and tribulations were. The figure appears as both light and man – having the appearance of Adam or Man. This vision became a typical image within Jewish mysticism and may well be the prototype for our present-day concept of the Christ figure.

Later, somewhere around 168 BC, the Book of Daniel calls this same figure the Son of Man and it is again found in the Gospels where it is referred to as the Glory of God. It is said that this being comes from heaven to the earthly realm, is incarnated in the man Jesus and eventually returns to the heavenly realm. It can thus be seen that the idea of a heavenly saviour or Redeemer was present prior to the Christian era.

Greek scholar and translator Gilbert Murray sums up the importance of Gnosticism at that time very neatly:

> The Gnostics are still commonly thought of as a body of Christian heretics. In reality there were Gnostic sects scattered over the Hellenistic world before Christianity as well as after. They must have been established in Antioch and probably in Tarsus well before the days of Paul or Apollos. Their Saviour, like the Jewish Messiah, was established in men's minds before the Saviour of the Christians.

Professor Bousset, theologian, author and one of Murray's researchers comments:

> If we look close the result emerges with great clearness, that the figure of the Redeemer as such did not wait for Christianity to force its way into the religion of Gnosis, but was already present there under various forms.

We find that there were many Gnostic thinkers in that period. For example, the German scholar and author Paul Trejo draws our attention to this fact when he says:

> There were Gnostics in Greco-Roman academies, the (middle) Platonists, before Christ was born (i.e. Fugulus, Eudorus of Alexandria, Thrasyllus). These are the Pythagorising Platonists who, before Plotinus, held that Knowledge can be perfected when it communes with the Divine, the mysterious Divine. Cicero speaks of Figulus (45 BC), the spiritual one, who was a contemporary of Apollonius of Tyana, the miracle worker and spiritualist mystic, and also a Pythagorean.

In exploring the roots of Gnostic thought and its particular brand of mysticism we need to pay attention to the ideas and philosophies of the Pythagoreans and the Platonists. Middle Platonism, so named after Plato was, in the main, 'other-worldly' and religious. It taught the similarity of the soul with the Supreme Being and highlighted the difference between discursive reasoning and intuition. Trejo went on to say:

> It is as though the Middle Platonists sought to incorporate Mysticism into Plato's perfect logic. The East still had a strong hold on many old Romans, just as it does on many new Californians. The main idea is the enmity between flesh and spirit, and the need for a Mediator between them.

The idea of the need for mediation, a kind of bridge between the material world and the Divine is not such a strange one, for it is found in all major religions in one form or another. It is only when the individual has achieved a certain level of awareness or knowledge that he can function as a mediator, as a Way. Jesus himself suggests that 'No man cometh to the Father except by me'. By this statement he seems to be acknowledging his own awareness of himself as a divine channel.

Attitudes to Jesus and his divinity came to vary from sect to sect within Gnosticism. Most regarded him as a spreader of knowledge (*gnosis*) which would liberate men and women from the control of evil gods and, after death, would ease their path to the Supreme Being. Some groups believed that Christ was an insubstantial spirit that merely appeared to be human. These docetists (from the Greek *dokein*, to seem) argued that an emanation from the Supreme Being could not have been a child who suffered from the evil of the world and died in agony: he was much too spiritually grand for that. In other words, it was only the appearance of Jesus Christ that died and suffered. Other Gnostics believed that the resurrection actually happened before the crucifixion, when Jesus' spirit left his body.

The Position of Women

There was a common belief that Jesus had female as well as male disciples and the position of women in those times is an interesting one. The idea of a virgin birth had a potency of its own, particularly if we remember that to be a virgin did not always just mean that a person was sexually pure – it also meant 'dedicated to God' or 'unmarried'. Jesus, the son of God and the saviour of mankind, could thus be born in a state of grace to such a woman.

The virgin birth, incidentally, continued to cause theological difficulties for Christians until St Thomas Aquinas, in the medieval period, expounded the view that Mary's conception was tarnished and that it was God who had eliminated original sin in her. However, Duns Scotus, a thirteenth-century British theologian, averred the opposite: that Mary was born, lived and died free from original sin. This suggestion had to wait until 1854 for complete ratification, when Pope Pius IX declared dogmatically that:

> . . . at the first instance of her conception was preserved immaculate from all stain of original sin, by the singular

> grace and privilege granted her by Almighty God, through the merits of Christ Jesus, Saviour of mankind.

Mary was thus redeemed by her Son from the moment of her conception. Not until 1950 did Pope Pius XII issue the dogma that put the seal of purity on the Virgin Mary, and incidentally explains why her grave has never been identified – after she died, she was taken directly into heaven. He wrote:

> . . . the Immaculate Mother of God, the ever Virgin Mary, when the course of her earthly life was run, was assumed in body and soul to heavenly glory.

This was her right as the Mother of God, lest she be corrupted in any way.

In fact, the idea of a woman immaculately conceiving a hero or demigod is quite ancient and it appears in all religions with the exception of Judaism. The pre-Christian Roman Empire used the idea of virgin birth to acknowledge a man's divinity. Later, the concept degenerated into a commonplace title, a reward for outstanding individuals, rather like a life peerage in the present day Pythagoras, Plato and Alexander the Great were all thought to have been born as a result of divine intervention. They were, however, human.

Virgin birth was a concept that Gnostics could easily embrace, although they were more conscious of the possible negative effects of such an action. Emanation, the bringing forth of a being as opposed to the act of birthing, is central to their beliefs. Their take on the creationist myth is simple – some would say neat. Others would say that it was truer than all the classic creationist alternatives. In his book *Elements of Gnosticism*, Stuart Holroyd states:

> In the beginning there existed only the transcendent God,

> a male principle that existed for eternities in repose with a female principle, the Ennoia (Thought), until there emanated or was brought forth from their union the two archetypes Mind (male) and Truth (female). In turn these principles emanated others, in male-female pairs to the total of thirty, known as Aeons, who collectively constituted the divine realm, known as the Pleroma or Fullness. Of all the Aeons, only the first, Mind, knew and comprehended the greatness of the Father and could behold him, but the last and youngest Aeon, Sophia (Wisdom) became possessed of a passion to do so, and out of the agony of this passion and without the knowledge or consent of her male counterpart, she projected from her own being a flawed emanation.
>
> This abortion, the 'Demiurge', was the creator of the material cosmos and imagined himself to be the absolute God. The cosmos that he created consisted of a number of spheres, each of which is ruled over by one of the lower powers, the Archons, who collectively govern man's world, the earth which is the lowest of the spheres of the degenerate creation.

This Demiurge has been equated to Jehovah or Yahweh, the unnameable Hebrew God, revealed to Moses – liberator, leader, lawgiver, receiver of revelations and historian – in the burning bush on Mount Horeb. The name JVH in Hebrew translates as 'He who is' which seems in some ways to correspond to the idea of a despotic creator god said to be all-knowing, ever-present and all-powerful. Moses is thought by some to have been the Egyptian government's Minister of the Colonies who, for the sake of regional peace and quiet, was prepared to go as far as inventing the story of the burning bush and the Jewish religion. He told the people:

> Obey all the laws that I am teaching you, and you will live and occupy the land which the Lord, the God of your ancestors, is giving you. Do not add anything to what I command you, and do not take anything away. Obey the commands of the Lord your God that I have given you. (Deuteronomy 4: 1–2)

Moses may or may not have enjoyed a high status but Sigmund Freud went even further in *Moses and Monotheism*, his anthology of essays, by suggesting that he was not a Jew, monotheism was an Egyptian heresy that he taught to the Jews when they left Egypt and Jehovah (Yahweh) was a bloodthirsty volcano god whose religion, adapted from that of the Midianite Arabs in western Arabia, was adopted after the exodus from Egypt. This god was also extremely arrogant, and apparently put paid to polytheism (multiple gods).

> No god was formed before me, nor will be after me. I, I am Yahweh, there is no other saviour but me. (Isaiah 45: 21)

Heresy

Gnostics have been accused of heresy right from the very beginning, but we can only begin to see how gnosticism fits into the scheme of religious thought when we move away from the idea that heretical views are solely held in opposition to the Christian religion.

Heresy, as defined today, is the holding of a belief that is in fundamental disagreement with the established teachings or doctrines of an organized religion. However, looked at in that way, heresy is a value judgment, based on an opinion of which faction is the established Church at any one time. Actually, the word comes from the Greek word *hairesis*, which is transliterated into English as the word 'heresy'. It literally means 'one who chooses'. The implication is 'one who asserts his own choice above God's Word' yet it also has the meaning of one who chooses what to believe – that is, one who makes a conscious choice. So Christianity itself could be perceived as being a heresy from the Jewish perspective.

The fact that most Gnostics make a conscious choice, based on an inner knowing of the Divine, suggests that they are only heretical in the original meaning of the word. Belief in the divine mysteries, with each person, of necessity, having their own individual approach to those mysteries, meant that there was no structured process which could be quantified as being common practice. This could be one of the reasons why Christianity, once it became organized, took precedence over gnosticism.

When a common practice is developed within a religion it lends credence to that practice. Some Christian Gnostics came to believe in chastity. These were the elect, known as the 'perfected'. They ate no meat because they believed that the wicked were transmigrated into the bodies of animals. However, they did eat fish, because they believed that sexual intercourse played no part in the reproduction process of aquatic animals. Their vegetarianism was pretty close to what we would recognize today as vegan, for they denied themselves eggs, cheese and milk as well. There is the story of a man who defended himself against the charge of heresy by saying he could not be a Gnostic because he lied, swore, ate meat and was a good Catholic.

The attitude of some Gnostics to sex and sexual congress is either enlightened or perverse depending on your point of view. Marriage, some of them argued, was worse than adultery because, in philosopher Bertrand Russell's words, 'it is continuous and complacent'. But at least their attitude was more complicated and diverse, more individualistic, than that set out in both the Old and the New Testaments.

Ultimately, part of the problem with the Gnostic thought that was experienced by the later orthodox Christians was the Gnostic insistence on the status of the female as God's equal. Whether this is because the world at the time of the early Christians was becoming more patriarchal is unclear. It probably also had a great deal to do with various perceptions of a woman's ability down through the ages and the belief that in some way she was inevitably flawed.

Even as late as 1991, *The Book of J,* written as a commentary by literary critic Dr Harold Bloom, with translations of the Pentateuch, the five books of Moses, by David Rosenberg, caused some controversy by not only suggesting that the earliest biblical texts had been written by a woman and were literary rather than religious but that later writers also imposed what is now accepted as an unchanging Jewish dogma.

Actually, much knowledge was lost or disregarded in gathering together the canon of writings which later became the New Testament. Only now is this knowledge slowly being recovered and interpreted from texts unearthed in recent times. As Elaine Pagels writes in her book *The Gnostic Gospels*:

> Every one of the secret texts which Gnostic groups revered was omitted from the canonical collection and branded as heretical by those who called themselves orthodox Christians. By the time the process of sorting the various writings ended – probably as late as the year 200 – virtually all the feminine imagery for God had disappeared from orthodox Christian tradition.

The place of the feminine element is an extremely important aspect of the understanding of Gnostic thought and we shall explore this in some depth in Chapter Seven. It must be stressed that Gnosticism did not turn out to be an alternative to paganism, Judaism or Christianity. Gnosticism enjoyed an early surge in some places, particularly in Alexandria, where the Jewish and Greek intellectual and spiritual worlds met, becoming an addition to or an accompaniment of, in one way and another, all the theologies that could be found there – very much the same thing happened with Islam, several centuries later. Put another way, Gnosticism might be said to differ from dogmatic or revelatory religions – those that enforce a body of doctrine published either in a Bible, a Koran, a Gita or other expository texts – in that its inspiration, essence and knowledge come from within the individual. With this degree of what some might call elitist individualism, it is not surprising that there sometimes seem to be as many Gnostic theologies as there are men and women who subscribe to them!

Diversity within Gnostic Sects

It was this very diversity that presented such a threat to those people who saw themselves as orthodox (straight-thinking) Christians. We shall look at some of those Gnostic sects and their leaders in greater detail in due course, but it is worthwhile highlighting some of their differences:

- Simon Magus, who lived contemporaneously with the apostles, used exorcisms and incantations, love-potions and charms. He maintained that much scripture, particularly the Old Testament, was a collection of allegories. He is held by many not to be truly Gnostic.
- Menander used magic to overcome the angels, and believed that only if you were baptised into the cult could you obtain eternal youth.
- The Ebionites believed that Jesus was just a man. They believed in the Messianic character of Jesus, but denied his divinity and supernatural origin. They observed all the Jewish rites, such as circumcision and the seventh-day Sabbath; they only accepted the Matthew gospel and maintained that Paul was an apostate because he had previously rejected Christianity and, in addition, practised Jewish customs.

- Nicolaitanes practised adultery and ate sacrifices meant for idols. They became obscene as well as Gnostic.
- Carpocrates believed in magic and taught that fornication was in order. He and his followers maintained that human beings are confined in a series of reincarnations by creator angels, but will eventually break free. They also believed that Jesus despised Jewish laws but his divinity protected him from them. Jude, servant of Jesus Christ and brother of James, is believed to be taking on Carpocrates when he wrote:

> For there are certain men crept in unawares, who were before of old ordained to this condemnation, ungodly men, turning the grace of our God into lasciviousness, and denying the only Lord God, and our Lord Jesus Christ . . . These be they that separate themselves, sensual, having not the Spirit.

- Cerinthus too believed that Jesus was just a man and that Christ was baptised into him and departed before the crucifixion.
- Saturninus thought he was an angel and one of the 'perfected' (see above). He thought Jesus was created to destroy the evil Jewish god. Sex, marriage and reproduction were sinful because they came from Satan.
- Marcus believed in transubstantiation, the idea that if the Holy Spirit put a drop of blood into wine and blessed it, the drinker would understand the mysteries of the universe and the prophetic.
- Marcion rejected the Old Testament and believed its god to be the author of sin. He was heavily reliant on astrology and he thought there was no resurrection and that Jesus was a phantom.
- Tatian (not the Venetian painter) believed that Adam was damned, wine was sinful, the soul vanished with the body and medicine is demonic.

- Ophites worshipped the serpent as the source of forbidden knowledge: The Sethians saw themselves in a direct line from Seth who was born of Adam and Eve and started the human race. Adam, it is claimed, warned them about the coming flood and an imminent conflagration of the world. The Peratae believed that Jesus was the son of the serpent. The Naasseni worshipped the serpent, thought their order was started by Jesus' brother James, believed that Adam was hermaphroditic and enjoyed orgies.
- Cainites fervently worshipped Cain, the son of Adam and Eve. He was regarded as a victim of the evil angel, along with Esau, while Abel and Jacob were considered to be intrinsically wicked. Cainites regarded it as a duty to break Jehovah's laws because he was an oppressor.
- Apelles believed that Jesus was flesh which disintegrated after the resurrection.
- Calistus started a commune that allowed fornication, common law marriages, drug-induced sterility and abortions but claimed boastfully 'No true Christian does these things'.
- Elchasaites believed that Jesus had been made flesh many times, and they busied themselves with mathematics, astrology and sorcery. Alcibiades started the Elchasai; they believed in female angels, remission of sins and the practice of circumcision.
- According to Basilides, man can be born without original sin, evil spirits enter us and force us to sin, baptism neutralizes involuntary sin but voluntary sin can only be purged by penance. 'We are no longer Jews', he said, 'and not yet Christians'. He also believed that Simon of Cyrene was crucified instead of Jesus when Simon took on the appearance of Jesus.
- Valentinus believed that only the acolytes of Sophia are predestined to be saved and that they do not need to perform good works. His followers also admitted a Jewish origin: the remark 'When we were Hebrews we were orphans' is typical.

By the time the Christians were beginning to organize themselves and become an accepted religion for the masses, several other heresies came into being that were not necessarily Gnostic (that is, gained from personal experience). Some of these are:

Adoptionism
Christ was a fully flesh-and-blood human being – not pre-existent or, for most adoptionists, born of a virgin. Christ was apparently not born the Son of God, but was adopted as such at some point later in his life (his baptism, his resurrection, etc.).

Appollinarianism
This is the heresy debated at the Council of Constantinople I (AD 381) which asserts that Jesus was not fully human. He was believed to be fully divine and therefore could not at the same time be fully human. The essence of the belief was that Christ had a human body and a human sensitive soul but no human rational mind, for the Divine Logos had taken its place.

Docetism
This was the teaching that Jesus only *appeared* to be a man, but was really some kind of angel or spirit being. According to the doctrine of the two natures, which was established at the Council of Chalcedon in 451 when a number of perceived heresies were dealt with:

> We teach . . . one and the same Christ, Son, Lord, Only-begotten, known in two natures, without confusion, without change, without division, without separation.

This supposedly corrected the error by asserting that Christ was 100 percent man. Interestingly, most Christians, because of their understanding of the orthodox position that Jesus the man is somehow also 'God', seem to persist in what J.A.T. Robinson calls a 'supranaturalistic' view of Christ.

In fact, popular supranaturalistic Christology has always been dominantly docetic. That is to say, Christ only appeared to be a man or looked like a man because 'underneath' he was still God.

Nestorianism

This is the view held by Nestorius, which was debated at the Council of Ephesus in AD 431. This view held that Christ is composed of two separate 'persons', the first a 'God person' and the other a 'human person'. Nestorianism was condemned and the 'orthodox' belief that Christ was one person, both 100 percent God and 100 percent man, was upheld. However, it was this type of belief that was taken to the East and it became incorporated into attempts to convert the Chinese people.

Any religion tries to forge and explain links with what might be called Divine energy – mystery religions play their part in allowing this to happen. Gnosticism, whether Christian or otherwise, takes its place in this category by claiming special knowledge of the Divine.

Chapter Two:

Mystery Religions

In order to understand what have become known as mystery religions, we have first to comprehend the place that was held by worship in simpler times. It was, first and foremost, a series of traditions and rites – usually a collection of regional practices to honour the local gods. The majority of people were resistant to the idea of any sort of innovation that would affect the practices that they had accepted – in particular, those that they believed were working for them and were acceptable to their gods.

Many of the gods in these polytheistic societies of the Hellenistic (Greek-speaking) times were initially vegetation gods, personalizations of qualities that were needed to help the people achieve what might today be called a sustainable lifestyle. In Greece, different deities were worshipped in different cities: in Athens it was Athena: in Sparta it was Artemis; in Corinth Aphrodite held sway and so forth. In the Roman provinces it was very similar and there was a great deal of cross-fertilization of ideas and principles between a number of cultures.

In Greece, temples were places where animal sacrifices were made, for all gods were perceived as having their own preference – their own sacred animal. In particular rites, certain parts of the animals were more favoured than others. There was perhaps also a good deal of 'laissez faire' for – provided that they had respect for the gods – the believer held the faiths of his neighbours to be just as important as his own.

The Roman way of worship was to recognize that sacrifices to the gods brought rewards. Public veneration was seen as pleasing the gods so that they would send rain, good harvests, military victories and other necessary public blessings. Private sacrifice was offered in order to achieve more personal goals: people were simply taught to pray according to a certain formula.

Those whose spiritual aspirations were not satisfied by the public worship of the gods could turn to the contemplation of higher mysteries. There was a sense of kinship – a sense of belonging to a community of like-minded people and of being singled out for special knowledge, together with an ongoing sense of knowledge still to be revealed and the promise of a life beyond the mundane.

Mystery religions, as this contemplation later came to be called, all have different features but they also tend to have certain points in common. These include:

- *An initiation ceremony* which is some form of cleansing, a ritual bath, or baptism. This act signifies the letting go of the previous life and a welcoming into the new, whether that is a new way of thinking, acting or being. Even in early times the initiate had to be introduced by other members.
- *A ritual meal,* shared on a regular basis by adherents to the belief. This breaking of bread together is a celebration of community and a way of cementing a sense of brotherhood and common purpose. Transubstantiation is often a feature of these meals when an ordinary mundane substance takes on a highly religious or esoteric significance. This probably has its roots in the early shamanic practices when people believed that the shamans or priests would take on the qualities of the animal or plant they were ingesting.

- *Miraculous or remarkable birth and death* experienced by the instigator of the religion. Such belief had a great deal to do with ideas of divinity. We have already seen how the idea of virgin birth was accepted in earlier times and as we study the creation myths we will come to see how people needed to understand the transition from the sacred or divine to the secular world. Gods or religious leaders in some of the earlier mystery religions were seen literally as descending into matter.
- *Restoration to life at death,* or on what appears to be death. The religious leader is restored to life but ultimately ends up in heaven, thus proving his divinity. A 'dying-and-rising' god is one of the oldest motifs in religious thought as seen in the Babylonian story of Dammuz and Innana which tells the myth of Innana's descent into the underworld, later to be rescued by Dammuz. Often, the 'death' was simply a visit and return to the underworld, and much later was treated as symbolic. As a matter of interest, this principle of the dying God is still celebrated in the Cycle of the Year by modern-day Pagans.
- *A female principle* or Divine Mother image, which is often very strong. Sometimes she is depicted as Mother Earth or as a Consort, but is always given her rightful place as Progenitor. We shall see more of this idea when we consider the creation myths.
- *Arcane knowledge* that is imparted by the divine man to his followers while he is living, although he is often ridiculed.This is a feature of those religions which required initiation, for each successive initiation brought more hidden knowledge.

The Roots of Gnosticism

Because the roots of Gnosticism are so buried in antiquity it has always been difficult to ascertain how it first began to develop. It is possible however to draw comparisons with other religions which were in existence at the time and to hazard an educated guess as to where there was perhaps cross-fertilization.

Zoroastrianism

Zoroastrianism is an ancient oral religion founded, it is thought, by the prophet Zarathushtra (known to the Greeks as Zoroaster) in about 1200 BC. It is a religion that attempts to make sense of the spiritual mysteries and though it does not qualify on all the points mentioned above, it could be called a mystery religion. It is considered by some to be the earliest monotheistic view to have evolved among mankind. The Wise Lord, Ahura Mazda or God of Light, is the good god. He is opposed by Angra Mainyu (also called Ahriman) who, according to some traditions, is his twin brother. This of course gives a dualistic twist to the myths that reflect the conflict between good and evil. According to Zoroastrianism, the Earth was created by Ahura Mazda as a battlefield on which to fight Angra Mainyu.

Zoroastrianism was the dominant world religion during the time of the Persian empires (559 BC to AD 651) and was, therefore, perhaps the most powerful world religion at the time of Jesus. It is thought to have had a major influence on all other religions of its time, particularly Judaism and Christianity, as well as later religions, and also on the beliefs that are central to these religions. Zoroastrianism is still practised on a worldwide basis today, especially in areas of Iran and India.

The *Gathas* (principle hymns) are an integral part of Zoroastrianism and their importance cannot be emphasized enough. As the *Tao Te Ching* is to Taoism, so they are the centrepiece of scripture and inspiration. The *Gathas* are also somewhat enigmatic and obscure and other scriptures contain lengthy commentaries on them. Mary Boyce in her book *Zoroastrians, Their Religious Beliefs and Practices* says:

> These are not works of instruction, but inspired, passionate utterances, many of them addressed directly to God; and their poetic form is a very ancient one, which has been traced back (through Norse parallels) to Indo-European times. It seems to have been linked with a mantic tradition, that is, to have been cultivated by priestly seers who sought to express in lofty words their personal apprehension of the divine; and it is marked by subtleties of allusion, and great richness and complexity of style.

Although a number of Gnostic scholars have concluded that there is little to link Gnosticism with Zoroastrianism, it can be seen that the 'personal apprehension of the divine' is common to both. Another aspect which may also link them is in the use of magic and magical practices.

When the Persian Empire collapsed and Greek culture began to take over there was obviously a good deal of fear and confusion in their known world. Dr M.D. Magee writes:

> Fall of empire and destruction of religion left large numbers of Persian Magi unemployed . . . They had to earn a crust and were thrown on their own skills and inventiveness to do it. The Magi knew a lot of tricks they had used to impress the Persian faithful, and they adapted these to their wider Greek, and then Roman audiences.

With apparently little comprehension of magical practice he continues:

> These were the foundations of magic – conjuring tricks and sleight of hand used by the Magi to attract audiences in the market places where they would then explain to a gawping crowd their popular distortions of Zoroastrianism. They

> became travelling magicians but they were lucky enough to have a mass of increasingly superstitious people to gull, and attracted small groups of disciples.

What he is actually writing about is what is today known as thaumaturgy. The word comes from the Greek word '*thaumatourgos*' which means 'miracle working' – from *thauma* (marvel) and *ergos* (work). Thaumaturgy is the use of magic for non-religious purposes; the art or science of 'wonder working'; using magic to change things on the Earth Plane. It is sometimes referred to as 'low magic'. It does not have the negative associations of words such as sorcery or necromancy because it originally referred to the production of wonders for positive ends rather than any intent to cause someone harm.

It is quite true that there are those Magi who would have been thrown back on their own resources, but Dr Magee continues somewhat judgmentally:

> These unemployed Magi would have spread the dark idea that the world was evil, based on their own background religion and fall from grace.

However, he does go on to contend that:

> Their disciples, influenced then by Greek culture over subsequent generations, founded Hellenistic Magic, Gnosticism, the Hermeneutica, perhaps Essenism and ultimately Christianity. Hybridisation of them in the first two centuries AD gave a variety of Christian Gnostic cults that the Roman church picked on as its first heretics and drove into impotence if not extinction by the end of the third century.

Those systems of belief which continued to use magical practice would no doubt have used what is now called theurgy, which is the use of magic for religious or self-development purposes. It is often referred to as 'high magic', and is considered to be the best use of magic as it calls on the powers of God or the gods and is generally geared towards the good of others. We see one use of such powers in the turning of water into wine at the wedding in Canaan by Jesus, who is believed to have spent a period of time with the Essenes, an ancient Jewish ascetic sect.

Since time immemorial, poetry has been used as a vehicle to enhance perception. Indeed, Mary Boyce says of Zarathustra and his poetry:

> Such poetry can only have been fully understood by the learned; and since Zoroaster believed that he had been entrusted by God with a message for all mankind, he must also have preached again and again in plain words to ordinary people. His teachings were handed down orally in his community from generation to generation, and were at last committed to writing under the Sasanians, rulers of the third Iranian empire. The language then spoken was Middle Persian, also called Pahlavi; and the Pahlavi books provide invaluable keys for interpreting the magnificent obscurities of the Gathas themselves.

We can see that in the oral transmission of hidden truths and in the belief in one God there are similarities in thought between Gnosticism and Zoroastrianism. When we come to look in Chapter Eight at alchemy – which might be considered to be one aspect of Gnosticism – we shall see similarities in the use of so-called 'magical' or spiritual powers.

The Worship of Dionysus

Originally Dionysus was said to be a Thracian god, whose followers practised fertility rites, lusted for liquor – it is claimed that Dionysus, known by the Romans as Bacchus, invented wine, thereby releasing the secret of the grape – and enjoyed tearing wild animals apart and eating them raw. This rite was probably an act of transubstantiation – making food sacred and ingesting power – whether that of the animals or of the god himself.

There are a number of stories in existence about Dionysus' birth. He is supposed to be the son of the Greco-Roman supreme god Zeus and his mistress Semele (Phrygian goddess of the earth, the Earth Mother) or alternatively of Zeus and Persephone (Queen of the Underworld). When just a baby, he was ripped to pieces by the Titans as an act of revenge. Only his heart was saved, which was either swallowed by Zeus, stitched into the god's thigh to preserve the baby or given back to Semele who had been recovered from the dead after a trick played by Zeus' wife, the goddess Hera. In any event he was born again, thus fulfilling the criterion of the Divine Child. For this he received the name Dithyrambos (he of the double doors).

He is usually pictured carrying a thyrsus – a staff covered in pine cones, ivy leaves and vines, which are all plants sacred to him. When Dionysus grew up he discovered how to cultivate the vine and how to extract the fruit's precious juice. Hera, in yet another fit of anger, struck him with madness – or intoxicated him – forcing him to wander through various parts of the earth. To make amends, the goddess Rhea, mother of Zeus, taught him her religious rites, thus healing him; he then set out on a journey through Asia teaching people the cultivation of the vine.

This journeying is, of course, representative of the pilgrimage that the seeker after knowledge must make in order to find himself. Divine Madness and the dangers inherent in the unbridled passion that is seen at a distance in the Dionysian worship have a seductiveness all of their own. This, when tamed, becomes an awareness of the higher mysteries and the euphoria of their discovery.

Bertrand Russell sums up the attraction of Dionysus in his *History of Western Philosophy*:

> His worship in the original form was savage, and in many ways repulsive. It was not in this form that it influenced the philosophers but in a form which was ascetic, and substituted mental for physical intoxication . . . The worshipper of Dionysus reacts against prudence. In intoxication, physical or spiritual, he recovers an intensity of feeling which prudence had destroyed; he finds the world full of delight and beauty, and his imagination is suddenly liberated from the prison of everyday preoccupations. The Bacchic ritual produced what was called 'enthusiasm', which means, etymologically, having the god enter into the worshipper, who believed that he became one with god. Much of what is greatest in human achievement involves some element of intoxication, some sweeping away of prudence by passion. Without the Bacchic element, life would be uninteresting; with it is dangerous. Prudence versus passion is a conflict that runs through history. It is not a conflict in which we ought to side wholly with either party.

It is obvious from many of the stories in existence that there was a distinctly negative side to the worship of Dionysus. The lack of control and the licentiousness of the rites was not easily understood except perhaps in the context of what today would be called an altered state of consciousness. The mass hysteria which often accompanied the rites was of concern to the authorities and – as it was the women who were apparently most affected – it obviously posed a threat to the status quo.

According to the *Encyclopaedia Britannica*:

> As Dionysus apparently represented the sap, juice or lifeblood element in nature, lavish festal orgia (rites) in his honour were widely instituted. These Dionysia (Bacchanalia) quickly won converts among the women in the post-Mycenaean world. The men, however, met it with hostility. According to tradition, Pentheus, king of Thebes, was torn to pieces by the bacchantes when he attempted to spy on their activities, while the Athenians were punished with impotence for dishonouring the god's cult. The women, nevertheless, abandoned their families and took to the hills, wearing fawn skins and crowns of ivy and shouting "Euoi!", the ritual cry. Forming thyasi (holy bands) and waving thyrsoi (fennel wands bound with vine leaves and tipped with ivy), they danced by torchlight to the rhythm of the flute and the tympanon (kettle drum).

Once again, the women seem to allow themselves to be possessed by the spirit of the god:

> While they were under the god's inspiration, the bacchantes were believed to possess occult powers, the ability to charm snakes and suckle animals, as well as preternatural strength that enabled them to tear living victims to pieces before indulging in a ritual feast (omophagia). The bacchantes hailed the god by his titles of Bromios (Thunderer), Taurokeros (Bull-horned) or Tauroprosopos (Bull-faced), in the belief that he incarnated the sacrificial beast.

Orpheus is supposed to have made the Dionysian cult respectable enough to influence Orphism.

Orphism

Orphism was sufficiently influential to become acceptable – first to Pythagoras, then to Plato and thence into most subsequent philosophy. Its ideas also permeated later Christian theology. There is some doubt as to whether or not Orpheus was simply a mythical being who did not exist outside the fantasies of pre-Christian storytellers such as Homer and Virgil.

G.R.S. Mead describes him thus:

> . . . few know the importance that mythical Orpheus plays in Grecian legends, nor the many arts and sciences attributed to him by fond posterity. Orpheus was the father of the pan-Hellenic faith, the great theologer, the man who brought to Greece the sacred rites of secret worship and taught the mysteries of nature and of God. To him the Greeks confessed they owed religion, the arts, the sciences, both sacred and profane . . . therefore . . . it will be necessary to treat of a theology which was first mystically and symbolically promulgated by Orpheus, afterwards disseminated enigmatically by Pythagoras, and in the last place scientifically unfolded by Plato and his genuine disciples.

In myth, Orpheus was the son of Calliope (which means 'beautiful voice'), the Muse of eloquence and epic or heroic poetry, and either Oeagrus, a Thracian king, or the god Apollo. His songs could charm wild beasts and coax even rocks and trees into movement. It was said to be Orpheus' music which prevented the crew of the Argos from being lured to destruction by the Sirens – who falsely promised that they would give knowledge, ripe wisdom and a quickening of the spirit to every man who came to them.

Legend has it that Orpheus visited the underworld and confronted Hades, after charming the ferryman Charon, the guard dog Cerberus and the three judges of the dead with his music in an attempt to rescue his wife, Eurydice, who had been killed by a snakebite when running away from Aristaeus, a shepherd who had made advances to her. Orpheus convinced the gods of the underworld that they should let her go by seducing them with beautiful music, but he lost her for ever when he disobeyed their instructions to trust that Eurydice would follow him. He looked back on the way out, whereupon she slipped back and ended up in the underworld as a spirit. Given that the Greek word *orphnei* may mean darkness or the underworld, the story makes sense and such a visit, of course, is one of the requirements of a mystery religion.

The story ended dramatically with Orpheus vowing to have nothing more to do with women (that is, to remain celibate) – an unfortunate act of self-denial that opened the door into darkness again. He ended up by being torn to pieces by a mob of crazed Thracian women in a Dionysian (Bacchic) orgy of religious and drink-induced ecstasy. In his volume on the Greek myths Robert Graves says:

> When Dionysus invaded Thrace, Orpheus neglected to honour him, but taught other sacred mysteries and preached the evil of sacrificial murder to the men of Thrace, who listened reverently. Every morning he would rise to greet the dawn on the summit of Mount Pangaeum, preaching that Helius, whom he named Apollo, was the greatest of all gods. In vexation, Dionysus set the Maenads upon him at Deium in Macedonia. First waiting until their husbands had entered Apollo's temple, where Orpheus served as a priest, they seized the weapons stacked

> outside, burst in, murdered their husbands and tore Orpheus limb from limb. His head they threw into the river Hebrus, but it floated, still singing, down to the sea, and was carried to the island of Lesbos.

To some scholars, Orpheus the man, rather than the myth, acquired a reputation as a religious reformer who helped to ameliorate the effects of the alcoholic and sexual enthusiasms of Dionysus. The chief teachings of the Orphic cult are of reincarnation, a Greek version of the evils of bodily impurity, and a history of the universe which was formed by Cronos, who was later supplanted by his son Zeus. In this history Cronos formed an egg and created the first king of the gods, Phanes.

Phanes is the golden winged Primordial Being who was hatched from the shining Cosmic Egg that was the source of the universe. Called variously Protogonos (First-Born) and Eros (Love) – being the seed of gods and men – Phanes actually means 'Manifestor' or 'Revealer', and is related to the Greek words for 'light' and 'to shine forth.'

An ancient Orphic hymn addresses him thus:

> Ineffable, hidden, brilliant scion, whose motion is whirring, you scattered the dark mist that lay before your eyes and, flapping your wings, you whirled about, and through this world you brought pure light.

Other teachings of the Orphic cult are that the body is the prison of the soul, animals were not to be killed or eaten, the good were to be rewarded while the evil were to be punished in Nether World and self-denial and seriousness in religious matters was *de rigueur*.

It can be seen that many of these teachings seem to be a reaction against the excesses of the Dionysian cult, yet as these perceptions were absorbed by those who were seeking knowledge they formed the basis of what was to become Gnostic thought. There is a distinct similarity between these teachings and those that came in the wake of the life of Jesus. The principle of the Divine or favoured child is clear in both, as is the idea that we all possess a Divine spark within us. The sacred meal is also evident, not least as a way of ingesting the power of the individual. The sacrificial death is also present as is a visit to the underworld. These classical Greco-Roman mystery cults gave us the term 'mysticism'. Perhaps the word came from *myein* (meaning 'to close the lips and eyes') and refers to the sacred oath of the initiates, the *mystes*, to keep secret the inner workings of their religion.

Mithras

Mithras is the Roman name for the Indo-Iranian god Mitra, or Mithra, as he was called by the Persians. Unusually, his rites seem to belong to more than one culture and he appears to have kept his mysteries hidden. Mitra is one of the Hindu gods: in the Vedic pantheon *Mitra* was (with *Varuna*) one of the two most important of the sovereign principles of the universe. He was praised in the *Rig Vedas* (holy scriptures) thus:

> 1. Mitra, when speaking, stirreth men to labour: Mitra sustaineth both the earth and heaven.
>
> Mitra beholdeth men with eyes that close not. To Mitra bring, with holy oil, oblation.
>
> 2. Foremost be he who brings thee food, O Mitra, who strives to keep thy sacred Law, Aditya.
>
> He whom thou helpest ne'er is slain or conquered, on him, from near or far, falls no affliction.

Mithra is a *yazatas* (minor deity) in the Zoroastrian pantheon under Ahura-Mazda. He is the god of the airy light between heaven and earth and is also associated with the light of the sun. Standing as he does between two worlds, he is a mediator god and deals with contracts. Mithra is the subject of *Yashts* (hymns) in the Zoroastrian *Avesta*, which is the text compiled during the Sassanian period (224–640 BC) of the Persian Empire to preserve the much older oral tradition.

Mitra/Mithra does not, however, seem to have had his own cult in either Hinduism or in Zoroastrianism. There is no evidence to suggest that the Zoroastrian worship of Mithra used the form of worship or the iconography found in the Roman cult of Mithras. The Mithraic mysteries arose in the Mediterranean world at exactly the same time as Christianity but the largest quantity of evidence for mithraic worship actually comes from the western half of the Roman empire, particularly from the provinces around the Danube River in Germany and from Rome and her port city, Ostia, in Italy.

There is little supporting textual evidence to show how the worship was carried out – we have only the wealth of archaeological evidence to help us. Mithraism was much favoured by the legionnaires of the Roman army and there is an argument that the cult was spread through the deployment of the army. In some ways it resembled a secret society rather than a religion. The study of the cult can give us valuable insight into the cultural dynamics that led to the rise of Christianity.

Meetings and worship took place in a temple, called a mithraeum, which was made to resemble a natural cave. The ceiling of the mithraeum was vaulted and often had crushed pottery adhering to it to imitate natural rock. Sometimes the ceilings were perforated to let shafts of light in. The mithraeum was intended to symbolize the dome of heaven, or the Cosmos, and to commemorate the birth of Mithras.

Mithraea were longer than they were wide. They were usually around 10–12m long and 4–6m wide and they were entered from one of the short sides. Roman dining couches, called *klinai* or *podia*, lined the long sides of the mithraeum, leaving a narrow aisle in between. At the end of this aisle, opposite the entrance, was the cult image – usually a carved relief but sometimes a statue or painting – of the central icon of Mithraism: the 'bull-slaying scene' in which the god of the cult, Mithras, accompanied by a dog, a snake, a raven and a scorpion, is shown killing a bull. We explain this scene in more detail below. Most mithraea had room for only thirty to forty members and only a few were actually large enough for a bull to be sacrificed inside.

The structure of the cult itself was hierarchical. Members seem to have gone through a series of seven initiations, each of which had a special symbol and a ruling planet. From lowest to highest, these grades were:

1. *Corax* (raven, under Mercury)
2. *Nymphus* (a word meaning male bride, or acolyte, under Venus)
3. *Miles* (the soldier, under Mars)
4. *Leo* (the lion, under Jupiter)
5. *Perses* (the Persian, under Luna, the moon)
6. *Heliodronus* (the Sun's courier, under Sol, the sun)
7. *Pater* (father, under Saturn)

Each grade would have required a certain level of knowledge and codes of conduct and since each planet is supposed to help develop certain qualities these were added to at each stage. The first three ranks were more introspective while by the fourth the initiate had become an adept. Those who reached the highest grade, *Pater*, could form their own congregation. Mithraea were quite small, so new congregations were probably founded on a regular basis when one or more members reached the highest grade. It seems to have been possible for a mithraic initiate to be a member of more than one cult but women were not permitted to become members. This rather rigid structure may go some way to explain why Mithraism ultimately had problems in surviving as a religion.

In each mithraic temple there was a central scene showing Mithras sacrificing a bull (often called a tauroctony). Mithras is clad in a tunic, trousers, cloak, and a pointed cap usually called a Phrygian cap, similar to those later seen during the French revolution. Under the bull a dog drinks the blood dripping from the wound and a scorpion attacks the bull's testicles. Often the bull's tail ends in wheat ears signifying fertility and a raven is perched on the bull's back. On the left stands a tiny male figure, Cautes, holding an upraised and burning torch. Above him, in the upper left corner, is the sun god, Sol, in his chariot. On the right there is another small male figure, Cautopates. He also holds a torch, this time pointing downwards which is sometimes, but not always, alight. These two attendant figures, dressed in the same way as Mithras, are said to show the way to heaven and hell respectively and, interestingly, can often be seen represented in modern versions of Tarot cards.

Above Cautopates in the upper right corner is the moon, Luna. The sun and the moon thus represent duality and Day and Night. This group of figures is almost always present, but there are variations, of which the most common is an added line of the signs of the zodiac over the top of the bull-sacrificial scene.

Nowadays, it is believed that each figure and element in the scene correlates to specific constellations, to the seven planets recognized by the ancient Romans and to the position of these planets in relation to the most important measurements in ancient astronomy. Such scenes may represent, in astrological terms, the ending of the Taurean age. In that case, the original cult may have been much older than it was first thought, since the ending of the Taurean age can be dated to some 2000 years before Christ. There are a number of bull-slaying stories such as that of Theseus and the Minotaur in existence and we have already seen that Dionysus was called 'Bull-faced'.

There are a number of themes in the decorations of the mithrae. The most common scenes show:

- Mithras being born from a rock, which often has a snake coiled about it – a theme similar to the story of Phanes
- Mithras dragging the bull to a cave, presumably to perform sacred rites
- Mithras and the sun god, Sol, banqueting on the flesh of the bull while sitting on its skin
- Plants springing from the blood and semen of the sacrificed bull, representing fertility rites
- Sol investing Mithras with the power of the sun, for his role as mediator
- Mithras and Sol shaking hands over a burning altar

It had been believed that the Earth was static until Greek scholar and astronomer Hipparchus discovered the precession of the equinoxes (a way of measuring the movement of the earth) between 146 BC and 130 BC. His discovery was to have far-reaching religious implications. A new force had been detected that was capable of shifting the cosmic sphere: was it not likely that this new force was a sign of the activity of a new god? Mithras was therefore presumed to be very powerful if he was able to rotate the heavens, thus 'killing the bull' or displacing Taurus as the reigning image in the heavens.

Our earliest concrete evidence for the Mithraic mysteries places their appearance in the middle of the first century BC: the historian Plutarch says that in 67 BC a large band of pirates based in Cilicia (a province on the south-eastern coast of Asia Minor) were practising the 'secret rites' of Mithras. The cult probably did not enjoy a wide membership until the middle of the second century AD. It has some of the hallmarks of a mystery, or perhaps, mystical religion – the strange birth, the initiations, the ritual meals, the consorting with the gods and the arcane knowledge. When this arcane knowledge became provable by mathematical and scientific means the cult lost its mystery, leaving only the myths behind. These myths are in the process of being rediscovered today.

Any interested party who chooses to explore the pre-Christian religions will find that the major competitors to Christianity were not just Mithraism, therefore, but a combined group of cults included under the general title of 'paganism'. Gnostic cults were those which claimed to have knowledge.

R. McWilson in *The Gnostic Problem – A Study of the Relations Between Hellenistic Judaism and the Gnostic Heresy* suggests that:

> On the other hand, Gnosticism was not without its good points. It provided to some extent an intermediate stage between paganism and Christianity, and many no doubt who had first been drawn by some form of Gnostic doctrine later entered the Church to be faithful Christians. Again, Gnosticism was an experiment in the performance of a task which had to be done – the accommodation of Christianity and Hellenistic culture. Its very errors were a warning to others, while it also forced the orthodox to consider seriously what was to be accepted, what rejected, in the philosophy of the contemporary world. When all is said, however, despite its Jewish and Christian elements, despite its contribution to Christian thought as an experiment in accommodation, despite the good intentions of some at least of its exponents, Gnosticism is not Christian, but a phase of heathenism.

If heathenism is accepted as being any of a number of religions other than Christianity, Judaism or Islamism, then Gnosticism might indeed be considered to be heathen. If however we accept that it is the pursuit of a knowledge of the divine then it belongs to the mystery religions. The esoteric knowledge it reveals withstands the test of time and gives us a foothold in the future. That same esoteric knowledge allows us to understand the myths of creation.

Chapter Three:

The Creation Myths

Within every system of belief there are stories and myths which attempt to explain how the Earth came into existence and, more importantly, how the human race began. There are several common themes in all such stories, as can be seen in the early Greek creation myths. Renowned Greek scholar Robert Graves writes about four of them, beginning with the Pelasgian myth which firstly states:

> In the beginning, Eurynome, the Goddess of All Things, rose naked from Chaos, but found nothing substantial for her feet to rest upon, and therefore divided the sea from the sky, dancing lonely upon its waves. She danced towards the south, and the wind set in motion behind her seemed something new and apart with which to begin a work of creation. Wheeling about, she caught hold of this north wind, rubbed it between her hands, and behold! the great serpent Ophion. Eurynome danced to warm herself, wildly and more wildly, until Ophion, grown lustful, coiled about those divine limbs and was moved to couple with her. Now the north wind, who is also called Boreas, fertilises; which is why mares often turn their hind quarters to the wind and

> breed foals without aid of a stallion. So Eurynome was likewise got with child.

The common themes in this myth are:

- From Chaos (or the undifferentiated) there is made a duality (the sky and the sea)
- From air or an airy quality something else is formed (the north wind becomes the serpent Ophion)
- From wild motion or passion (in this case dance) there arises 'a coupling'
- From this coupling is born the universe

To continue:

> Next she assumed the form of a dove, brooding on the waves and, in due process of time, laid the Universal Egg. At her bidding, Ophion coiled seven times about this egg, until it hatched and split in two. Out tumbled all things that exist, her children: sun, moon, planets, stars, the earth with its mountains and rivers, its trees, herbs and living creatures.

The Universal Egg is an image which appears in many creation myths and we have already seen something similar in the story of Mithras' birth, where he arose from a rock around which was coiled the serpent:

> Eurynome and Ophion made their home on Mount Olympus, where he vexed her by claiming to be the author of the Universe. Forthwith she bruised his head with her heel, kicked out his teeth, and banished him to the dark caves below the earth.

At this point there is righteous anger at Ophion's false claims and a subsequent banishment by Eurynome to the underworld. As a matter of interest, it is Ophion who was the inspiration for the Ophite pre-Christian Gnostic sects and for many other serpent myths:

> Next, the goddess created the seven planetary powers, setting a Titaness and a Titan over each. Theia and Hyperion for the Sun; Phoebe and Atlas for the Moon; Dione and Crius for the planet Mars; Metis and Coeus for the planet Mercury; Themis and Eurymedon for the planet Jupiter; Tethys and Oceanus for Venus; Rhea and Cronus for the planet Saturn.

Now we have the creation of male and female archetypes, powers which are set over the planets to guide and guard them.

> But the first man was Pelasgus, ancestor of the Pelasgians; he sprang from the soil of Arcadia, followed by certain others, whom he taught to make huts and feed upon acorns, and sew pig-skin tunics such as poor folk still wear.

Note, says Graves, that this theory of creation has no gods or priests and the prime mover is feminine. We should also note that the first humans are taught basic survival skills. We can also see this with the Olympian Creation Myth which argues:

> At the beginning of all things, Mother Earth emerged from Chaos and bore her son Uranus as she slept. Gazing down fondly at her from the mountains, he showered fertile rain upon her secret clefts, and she bore grass, flowers and trees, with the beasts and birds proper to each. The same rain made the rivers flow and filled the hollow places with water, so that lakes and seas came into being.

Graves' third account, which along with the fourth he calls 'philosophical', might also be called abstract or poetic. He says:

> Some say that Darkness was first, and from Darkness sprang Chaos. From a Union between Darkness and Chaos sprang Night, Day, Erebus and the Air.
>
> From a Union between Night and Erebus sprang Doom, Old Age, Death, Murder, Continence, Sleep, Dreams, Discord, Misery, Vexation, Nemesis, Joy, Friendship, Pity, the Three Fates and the Three Hesperides.
>
> From a Union between Air and Day sprang Mother Earth, Sky and Sea.
>
> From a Union between Air and Mother Earth sprang Terror, Craft, Anger, Strife, Lies, Oaths, Vengeance, Intemperance, Altercation, Treaty, Oblivion, Fear, Pride, Battle; also Oceanus, Metis, and the other Titans, Tartarus, and the Three Erinnyes or Furies.

In the above tale it is, of course, the pairing and the 'coupling' which is important. There is no giving birth: all of the Qualities 'spring' into existence.

In this final story, the elements Earth, Fire, Air (or rather upper air and lower air) and Water are put in order in an almost scientific way before the Act of Creation begins:

> Others say that the God of All Things – whoever he may have been, for some call him Nature – appearing suddenly in Chaos, separated earth from the heavens, the water from the earth, and the upper air from the lower. Having unravelled the elements, he set them in due order, as they are now found. He divided the earth into zones, some very hot, some very cold, others temperate; moulded it into

> plains and mountains; and clothed it with grass and trees. Above it he set the rolling firmament, spangling it with stars, and assigned stations to the four winds. He also peopled the waters with fish, the earth with beasts, and the sky with the sun, the moon and the five planets. Lastly he made man – who, alone of all beasts, raises his face to heaven and observes the sun, the moon, and the stars – unless it be indeed true that Prometheus, son of Iapetus, made man's body from water and clay, and that his soul was supplied by certain wandering divine elements, which had survived from the First Creation.

It is always necessary to take into account the fact that our understanding of another culture – in this case the Judaic and Greek ones – is coloured by the words of the translator and by the times in which he lives.

Genesis

Moving on to Genesis in the King James Version of the Bible we find the same basic story of several stages of creation. First there is division into Heaven and Earth – an upper realm and a lower, and a spirit 'moving' on the waters:

> In the beginning God created the heaven and the earth. And the earth was without form and void; and the darkness was on the face of the deep. And the spirit of God moved upon the face of the waters. And God said, Let there be light: and there was light. And God saw the light, that it was good: and God divided the light from the darkness. And God called the light Day, and the darkness he called Night. And the evening and the morning were the first day. And

> God said, Let there be a firmament, and divided the waters which were under the firmament from the waters which were above the firmament; and it was so. And God called the firmament Heaven. And the evening and the morning were the second day.

Then there is the creation of the earth itself, and the vegetation that grows on it:

> And God said, Let the waters under the heaven be gathered together unto one place, and let the dry land appear; and it was so. And God called the dry land Earth; and the gathering together of the water called the Seas: and God saw that it was good. And God said, Let the earth bring forth grass, the herb yielding seed, and the fruit tree yielding fruit after his kind, whose seed is in itself, upon the earth: and it was so. And the earth brought forth grass, and herb yielding seed after his kind, and the tree yielding fruit, whose seed was in itself, after his kind: and God saw that it was good. And the evening and the morning were the third day.

Next God turns his attention to his heavens, creates more light, which we would now recognize as the creation of the planets, and more firmly divides day from night, giving a greater and a lesser light, the Sun and the Moon:

> And God said, Let there be lights in the firmament of the heaven to divide the day from the night; and let them be for signs, and for seasons, and for days, and years. And let them be for lights in the firmament of the heaven to give light upon the earth: and it was so. And God made two great lights; the greater light to rule the day, and the lesser light to

> rule the night; he made the stars also. And God set them in the firmament of the heaven to give light upon the earth. And to rule over the day and over the night, and to divide the light from the darkness: and God saw that it was good. And the evening and the morning were the fourth day.

Next on the fifth day, we have the formation of all the creatures:

> And God said, Let the waters bring forth abundantly the moving creature that hath life, and fowl that may fly above the earth in the open firmament of heaven. And God created great whales and every living creature that moveth, which the waters brought forth abundantly after their kind, and every winged fowl after his kind: and God saw that it was good. And God blessed them saying, Be fruitful and multiply, and fill the waters in the seas, and let fowl multiply in the earth. And the evening and the morning were the fifth day. And God said, Let the earth bring forth the living creature after his kind, cattle and creeping thing, and beast of the earth after his kind: and God saw that it was good.

Now we have, as it were, a final check, before there is a last flourish as God creates man in his own image. However, it is not just man that he creates. According to the scripture 'male and female created he them'. There is always controversy over this act for it is not known for definite whether he created two beings or one man with two polarities:

> And God said, Let the earth bring forth the living creature after his kind, cattle and creeping thing, and beast of the earth after his kind: and God saw that it was good.
>
> And God said, Let us make man in our image, after our likeness: and let them have dominion over the fish of the

> sea, and over the fowl of the air, and over the cattle, and over all the earth, and over every creeping thing that creepeth upon the earth. So God created man in his own image, in the image of God created he him; male and female created he them. And God blessed them and God said unto them, Be fruitful and multiply, and replenish the earth, and subdue it: and have dominion over the fish of the sea and over the fowl of the air, and over every living thing that moveth upon the earth. And God said, Behold I have given you every herb bearing seed, which is upon the face of all the earth, and every tree, in the which is the fruit of a tree yielding seed; to you it shall be for meat . . . And God saw everything that he had made, and behold, it was very good. And the evening and the morning were the sixth day.

Arguments consistently rage over whether the phrase 'be fruitful and multiply' is meant in the sexual sense or not, and we shall deal with some of the issues of sexuality in Gnostic thought later.

It is interesting to note that at this stage God says 'Let us make man in our image'; then it is said 'So God created man in his own image.' Now we must decide if this is simply an error of transcription or is there information there for us. Certainly, just as in Taoism we find that 'one becomes two becomes three becomes ten thousand', here it is implied that everything must be increased and the earth must be replenished. Later, in Chapter 2 of Genesis, God is given the title 'the Lord God' after the seventh day – almost an enhanced status. Many modern scholars believe that there are two stories here or rather two ways of telling the same story.

In the New Testament in the Bible, we can come very close to an understanding of Gnostic thought, for in many ways the following is the shortest creation story ever. When we come to the Gospel according to St John we read in the first verse:

> In the beginning was the Word and the Word was with God and the Word was God.

Put simply, God and the Word coexist and are one and the same. God, or the Godhead as it has come to be called, is recognized as ineffable, immeasurable, self-contained, transcendental, perfect, tranquil, the source of all. In the fourth verse is written:

> In him was life and the life was the light of men.

We have seen in Chapter One that the transcendental God emanated (brought forth, not gave birth to) the Aeons in Gnostic belief, after union with his feminine principle. These Aeons reside in the Pleroma, the realm of Light distinguished from the lower or manifest creation and were all given particular tasks and realms of being to care for, particularly of redeeming spirit from the trappings of the material state.

Barbelo

Here at the beginning of a Gnostic scripture entitled *Trimorphic Protennoia* is said to speak the Voice of the Silence, the Thought, or the feminine principle of the Divine:

> I am Protennoia, the Thought that dwells in the Light. I am the movement that dwells in the All, she in whom the All takes its stand, the first-born among those who came to be, she who exists before the All. She (Protennoia) is called by three names, although she dwells alone, since she is perfect. I am invisible within the Thought of the Invisible One. I am revealed in the immeasurable, ineffable (things). I am incomprehensible, dwelling in the incomprehensible. I move in every creature.

This aspect, also known as *Barbelo*, is the higher principle, the creative Thought of the Supreme Parent, who may also descend to the earth plane for the purpose of the salvation of those below. According to this cosmology then, only the 'only begotten' first-born of the union between God and Protennoia actually understands the method of emanating. Sophia, the last and most presumptuous of the Aeons, tries to copy him in her passion to return to her Parent, but does not succeed in producing a genuine creation, only an 'abortion' which she names Ialdeboath. This is the demiurge, which then proceeds to create, in the belief that he is the true God.

This negative entity – who was the evil god of this world – proceeded to generate further entities and created man, in a sort of parody of the Genesis account of the creation of Adam. Stories seem to differ from here, for some say that Sophia was herself trapped in matter, others that she set about teaching her creation in order to put things right, yet others that she must ultimately unite with the Christ Light in order to redeem the World. In various myths and scriptures there follows a long drama in which the Aeons work to free the trapped Light from the grip of the lower powers, the creators and rulers of this inferior world.

Gnosticism is based on an intuitive knowledge of the divine and it is possible to see two important aspects of Gnostic thought in this story; and also how Gnostics would apply the ideas to themselves. The first aspect is Sophia's wish, which is akin to their own, to return to the Source of all things and to know and act as he did; the second is to account for the division between the spiritual realm and the physical.

In Chapter Two we saw that the belief that the physical existence has its roots in the fight between good and evil is rooted in Zoroastrianism, as is the idea that the Earth itself is a battleground. Zoroastrianism was the first religion to teach the idea that time is historical rather than cyclic, with a specific beginning (Creation) and an end. It taught of:

- a heaven and a hell
- a future Day of Judgment
- resurrection
- a Divinely ruled perfect world

These teachings had a considerable influence on the Jews from whom these concepts passed over into Christianity and later into Islam.

It is more than probable, therefore, that it was from the monotheistic Zervanism, a perhaps heretical branch of Zoroastrianism, that the Gnostic theory of the Aeons developed – with its idea of the Absolute as 'Eternity', from which proceed further emanations. In a sense then, Zervanism, and its contrast between the serene realm of light above and the world of conflict and contrast in the physical realm below, could now be called an early sect of Gnosticism.

The story of Ialdeboath, as an evil or uncaring god, made allowances for bad things happening because creation was seen as a mistake anyway. The Gnostics place the blame for all ills firmly in the hands of the demiurge. In many ways this idea is similar to the Buddhist belief that much of life, if not all, is simply illusion.

Gnostic Creation Myths

'Gnostic creation myths' according to Professor Hopkins (see Chapter One) 'drive their main points home by repetition, variety and mystification':

> Theirs is a drama in four grand acts: the creation of God, the creation of the universe, the creation of the first humans, and final salvation or damnation . . . Each historical act turns on a cycle of error, conflict, mutual misunderstanding and redemptive forgiveness. Each act repeats the basic message: some superior creatures,

> whether divine or human, have flawed elements of divinity trapped inside them. By magnifying the power of the divine, and by divine mercy, the best creatures can increase their potential to be saved. But this core message is repeatedly disguised in variant forms. Just as divinities replicate aspects of themselves, so Gnostic myths create their own voluptuous variety. There seems no end to the diversity, or to the ever-increasing complexity of the subordinate divinities, and their stories.

However, one important part in all of the Gnostic creation stories is that some of the pure spiritual nature, the 'divine spark', was planted in some souls. A redeemer was then sent from the divine world to reveal the way of escape out of the material world for this divine spark. The saved soul must pass through the realms of the world rulers (*archons*) in order to return to its proper spiritual home, so if that soul is among the elect it is easily able to do this. This hierarchy of salvation is a particularly important aspect of Gnosticism in the early Christian period.

Jewish Gnosticism

Before we look at Christian Gnosticism and its beliefs, we need to put the place of gnosticism into perspective prior to that period. We can do that by taking a brief look at Jewish gnosticism:

> There is no doubt that a Jewish gnosticism existed before a Christian or a Judeo-Christian gnosticism. As may be seen even in the apocalypses, since the second century BC gnostic thought was bound up with Judaism, which has accepted Babylonian and Syrian doctrine; but the relation of this Jewish gnosticism to Christian gnosticism may, perhaps, no longer be explained.

In the early Christian period, there was no school of thought of which the Jews had not been aware and some people would suggest that all heresies, including those of Gnosticism, arose ultimately from Judaism. Jewish mysticism and Jewish Gnostics, there is no doubt, existed prior to Christianity since the principal elements of gnosticism (intuited knowledge) were based on the speculations, explorations and questions of the Jewish mind.

Hebrew words and names of God, in fact, often provided the matrix for later gnostic systems. Magic was a highly important part of the doctrines and manifestations of gnosticism and it largely occupied Jewish thinkers. Such depth of thought gave rise to the Kabbalah as a spiritual discipline, which will be seen further on in the book. It is perhaps an interesting fact that many heads of gnostic schools and founders of gnostic systems were reviled as Jews by the later Church Fathers. When we review some of those schools, later in the book, we will be aware of the struggle to accommodate new thought into old ideas.

Plato

One other Gnostic type of creation story which has to be mentioned is, of course, that put forward by Plato. In his cosmological work *Timaeus,* the philosopher explains an innate separation between matter and spirit, giving us a very dualistic viewpoint. The Creator is thus seen to entrust the formation of man to a lesser entity than himself. In this Gutenberg translation, Timaeus summarizes Plato's own thoughts:

> As I said at first, all things were originally a chaos in which there was no order or proportion. The elements of this chaos were arranged by the Creator, and out of them he made the world. Of the divine he himself was the author, but he committed to his offspring the creation of the

> mortal. From him they received the immortal soul, but themselves made the body to be its vehicle, and constructed within another soul which was mortal, and subject to terrible affections: pleasure, the inciter of evil; pain, which deters from good; rashness and fear, foolish counsellors; anger hard to be appeased; hope easily led astray. These they mingled with irrational sense and all-daring love according to necessary laws and so framed man.

Plato then sets out the rationale behind the physical body in very understandable terms and warns:

> The truth concerning the soul can only be established by the word of God.
> Still, we may venture to assert what is probable both concerning soul and body.

Plato later differentiates between a 'mortal' soul and he who is training up the divine principle in himself – a concept which was adopted by the Gnostics in the 'divine spark' as we saw above. This concept also has a resonance with much of the teaching of the *Tao Te Ching,* where the teacher is called the sage, and equally with other Eastern religions as we now understand them:

> The divine soul God lodged in the head, to raise us, like plants which are not of earthly origin, to our kindred; for the head is nearest to heaven.
>
> He who is intent upon the gratification of his desires and cherishes the mortal soul, has all his ideas mortal, and is himself mortal in the truest sense. But he who seeks after knowledge and exercises the divine part of himself in godly

> and immortal thoughts, attains to truth and immortality, as far as is possible to man, and also to happiness, while he is training up within him the divine principle and indwelling power of order. There is only one way in which one person can benefit another; and that is by assigning to him his proper nurture and motion. To the motions of the soul answer the motions of the universe, and by the study of these the individual is restored to his original nature.

So in all of these creation myths we see the ways in which the minds of the people of the pre-Christian era worked and how they built their understanding. The Greek world also was intellectually turbulent. New ideas and ways of thinking were being put forward all the time. Of the time between Plato (428 to 7 BC), St Paul and the early Christian Gnostics, Gilbert Murray, the Greek scholar and translator speculates:

> This was the time when the Greek mind, still in its full creative vigour, made its first response to the twofold failure of the world in which it had put its faith, the open bankruptcy of the Olympian religion (the gods on Mount Olympus) and the collapse of the city state (like Athens).

He notes the change from care of the society or community to an introspection which has not been obvious before:

> Any one who turns from the great writers of classical Athens . . . to those of the Christian era must be conscious of a great difference in tone . . . The new quality is not specifically Christian: it is just as marked in the Gnostics . . . as in the Gospels . . . It is hard to describe. It is a rise of asceticism, of mysticism, in a sense, of pessimism; a loss of self-confidence, of hope in this life and of faith in normal

> human effort; a despair of patient inquiry, a cry for infallible revelation; an indifference to the welfare of the state, a conversion of the soul to God. It is an atmosphere in which the aim of the good man is not so much to live justly, to help the society to which he belongs and enjoy the esteem of his fellow creatures; but rather by means of a burning faith, by contempt for the world and its standards, by ecstasy, suffering and martyrdom, to be granted pardon for his unspeakable unworthiness, his immeasurable sins. There is an intensifying of certain spiritual emotions; an increase of sensitiveness, a failure of nerve.

This, you may think, is a pretty accurate analysis of the development of Gnosticism. Gilbert Murray continues with his exploration of the changes in the Greek systems of belief and their relevance to Gnosticism:

> . . . the whole tendency of Greek philosophy after Plato, with some illustrious exceptions . . . was away from the outer world towards the world of the soul. We find in the religious writings of this period that the real Saviour of men is not he who protects them against earthquake and famine, but he who in some sense saves their souls. He reveals to them the Gnôsis Theou, the Knowledge of God. The 'knowledge' in question is not a mere intellectual knowledge. It is a complete union, a merging of beings. And, as we always have to keep reminding our cold modern intelligence, he who has 'known' God, in a sense he is God . . .

So the scene is set for the coming of the Christ figure.

Chapter Four:

Gnosticism as Christian Heresy

There were so many changes taking place during the first centuries of what is now known as the Christian Era that it is difficult to differentiate between what was considered heretical and what was not. Christian gnostics, by and large, appeared to say the same things as other Christians, but they were much vilified because their rites were seen as incidents of depraved behaviour, their myths and doctrines as ridiculous and their intentions as apparently destructive to the true worship of God.

The early interaction of gnosticism and Christ is characterized by three periods in particular:

- the late first and early second centuries in which the foundations of Christian Gnostic traditions were laid at the time that the New Testament was being written.
- the mid-second to the early third century, the period of the great Gnostic teachers and systems. At that time Christian Gnostics claimed to possess the esoteric, spiritual interpretation of Christ's scriptures, beliefs and sacraments.
- the end of the second century into the fourth century, when there was a huge reaction against the teachings of Gnosticism.

It is difficult to decide whether gnosticism was actually a heresy in the first of the three periods, particularly as Christianity had not yet taken on its organized orthodox form. There were numerous interpretations and ideas about what Jesus said or meant. Probably the first person we should look at in this period is St Paul (Paul of Tarsus).

Paul of Tarsus

Many believe that Paul of Tarsus, whose letters were such a formative factor in the organization of orthodox Christianity, was actually Gnostic for he speaks of the Christ 'in' him, having received knowledge by direct revelation. On several occasions he is at pains to point out that although he met the apostles and elders he was not yet one of them. However, he received their blessing to preach to the Gentiles and to allow the latter to forgo circumcision.

In Acts 15: 28–29 the Church Fathers write to Paul's followers:

> For it seemed good to the Holy Ghost and to us to lay upon you no greater burden than these necessary things: That ye abstain from meats offered to idols and from blood, and from things strangled, and from fornication: from which if ye keep yourselves, ye shall do well. Fare ye well.

It might be assumed that there was some kind of initiation hierarchy within Christianity to begin with, since Paul designates himself as 'A servant of Jesus Christ, called to be an apostle' in the epistle to the Romans, although later in the second epistle to the Corinthians he calls himself 'Paul, an apostle of Jesus Christ'.

In Corinthians 2: 11 verse 10 he says:

> As the truth of Christ is in me . . .

Yet in verse 22 of the same chapter he admits his Jewish heritage by saying quite clearly:

> Are they Hebrews? so am I . . . Are they Israelites? so am I. Are they the seed of Abraham? so am I.

His ministry seems to have been to bring an understanding of the Christ Jesus to those not of his culture, therefore, which in theory means that he could be accused of heresy against his own faith, even if he could not exactly be called a Gnostic. His premise is that Divine righteousness is impartial. The status of Jew and gentile is shown to be equal, so that Abraham becomes the 'father of all who have faith' (Rom. 4: 11) rather than merely the progenitor of circumcised Jews.

In many ways, this shift in focus epitomizes the problem that so many researchers encounter when studying Gnosticism. In trying to make Gnosticism a religion in its own right the main point is lost – that direct experience of the Divine does not stop one from subscribing to a particular belief, culture or code of conduct. The Christos – the Spirit of Truth – is found after the union of mankind with the divine principle in him. The 'Christ principle', the awakened and glorified Spirit of Truth, is universal and eternal, and cannot be monopolized by any one person.

It was difficult for many of the powerful personalities of the time to sort out their personal viewpoints in relation to the accepted teachings of the Church. Valentinus, a Christian teacher and poet, also belongs to this first period of Christian Gnosticism.

Valentinus

If his ambition to be Pope had not been frustrated, Valentinus might well have made Christian theology develop in very different directions, even to the extent of giving rise to a form of Gnostic Christianity. Most of what is now known about his written work can be found in a fourth century Egyptian papyrus, called the Jung Codex. Named in honour of psychotherapist Carl Jung after its discovery in 1946, it contained translations of Valentinian texts into Coptic script. These texts were the first direct statement of Valentinus' beliefs that had been discovered outside the works of those who challenged him. The Codex also contained:

- the prayer of the apostle Paul
- the *Apocryphon of James* containing revelations of the risen Jesus to his brother
- the *Gospel of Truth*
- the *Epistle to Rheginos*, an expression of Paul's views on the Resurrection
- the *Tripartite Treatise*, probably written by Heracleon, on the subject of how the Spirit evolves, through the various stages of awareness, into Gnosis

We will look further at some of these works in Chapter Seven.

In many ways Valentinus has an impressive record of intellectual achievement. Born in Africa in about AD 100, possibly in Carthage, he was baptized a Christian. Educated in Alexandria, then a great centre of learning and Gnostic belief, he is thought have studied philosophy under the guidance of Theodas, who may in turn have been a pupil of St Paul. He was thirty-six when, during the papacy of Pope St Hyginus, he moved to Rome. The Pope's position of Bishop of Rome was the office that he really wanted, but in about AD 140 he lost the election by a small margin to a priest who claimed martyrdom.

Valentinus carried on his attempt to reconcile the dogmas of Gnosticism and Christianity while he worked as a priest and continued to live in Rome. For example, according to Irenaeus, who is now well known as a vociferous critic of Gnostic belief, he attempted to explain the Absolute, the Godhead, by saying that it was:

> perfect and pre-existent . . . dwelling in invisible and unnameable heights: this is the prebeginning and forefather and depth. It is uncontainable and invisible, eternal and ungenerated, is Quiet and deep Solitude for infinite aeons. With It was thought, which is also called Grace and Silence.

Some say that Valentinus published the conclusions on dogma that he reached in *The Gospel of Truth*. It appears that he remained a prominent and respected member of the Christian community and there is no evidence of him ever being actually accused of heresy – although it would seem that he was excommunicated. However, others believe that he may have left the Church after being passed over in Rome, taking up residence in Cyprus to continue his work. His influence, and perhaps presence, certainly led to the growth of schools of Gnosticism in Rome and Alexandria – which attracted many followers who represented a major threat to orthodox Christianity in the second and third centuries and for some time thereafter.

G.R.S. Mead, who has written widely about Gnosticism, highlights the enormity of Valentinus' task of reconciliation:

> The Gnosis in his hands is trying to . . . embrace everything, even the most dogmatic formulation of the traditions of the Master. The great popular movement and its incomprehensibilities were recognised by Valentinus as an integral part of the mighty outpouring; he laboured to weave all together, external and internal, into one piece, devoted his life to the task, and doubtless only at his death perceived that for that age he was attempting the impossible. None but the very few could ever appreciate the ideal of the man, much less understand it.

Remember that Gnosticism proposes two gods, one good, the other evil, with the latter controlling everything under the sun and redemption being possible only by *gnosis*: that is, esoteric knowledge. Irenaeus, one of Valentinus' sternest critics, actually quotes Valentinus on the nature of redemption:

> Perfect redemption is the cognition itself of the ineffable greatness: for since through ignorance came about the defect . . . the whole system springing from ignorance is dissolved in Gnosis. Therefore Gnosis is the redemption of the inner man; and it is not of the body, for the body is corruptible; nor is it psychical, for even the soul is a product of the defect and it is a lodging to the spirit: pneumatic (spiritual) therefore also must be redemption itself. Through Gnosis, then is redeemed the inner, spiritual man: so that to us suffices the Gnosis of universal being: and this is the true redemption.

Valentinus did not help his own cause long term by denying the original divinity of Jesus Christ, although he did revere him: which may have been his saving grace in the avoidance of the charge of heresy. The Valentinian tradition creates a sharp demarcation between the human and the divine aspects of Jesus. Valentinus and his followers believed that the human Jesus was born the true son of Mary and Joseph. When he went down into the water as he was baptized, the divine Saviour, referred to as the 'Spirit of the Thought of the Father', descended on him in the form of a dove and so, by a special dispensation, his body is at one with Sophia and her spiritual seed. This in the eyes of the Valentinians is the true virgin birth and resurrection from the dead, for He was reborn of the virgin Spirit.

In the recently translated Gnostic *Gospel of Truth*, it is argued that Jesus is indeed our Saviour, but in the sense of the Greek *soter,* meaning healer, and that his role was to cure us of ignorance of life's values, to revolutionize our belief in material things (lust, wealth. power, self-esteem) and to bring knowledge of the *pneuma* (literally breath of god): that is, the spirit to the soul and mind.

The attitude that Valentinus and his followers had to sex is also worth noting. They encouraged sex and marriage for spiritual people only, basing their belief on the *Gospel of John*:

> Whosoever is in the world and has not loved a woman so as to become one with her, is not out of the Truth, and will attain the Truth; but he who is from the world and unites with a woman, will not attain the Truth, because he made sex out of concupiscence alone.

This of course means that Valentinians never rejected marriage and raising children, since it meant that the seed of the spirit was spread more effectively. This placed some restriction on the coarser, unaware lower orders who could only know libido, and it makes Valentinus one of the few early Christians to espouse the joys of sexual intercourse so strongly.

Heracleon and Ptolemaeus

Two contemporaries of Valentinus (some say disciples), Heracleon and Ptolemaeus, also made contributions to Gnostic thinking. Very little is known about them except in the works of other people, which were mostly antagonistic to Gnosticism. Irenaeus names them both in his book *Against Heresies,* and describes their teachings as an 'abyss of madness and blasphemy against Christ'.

Clement of Alexandria, the gentler critic of Gnosticism, writes about Heracleon in his fourth book of *Stromata*, describing him as 'the most noted man of the Valentinian school'. He was one of the earliest – if not the first – to write an account of the New Testament.

Heracleon was also conservative about dogma and did his best to free it from oriental influences. In his commentary on the *Gospel According to St John*, he talked about the three levels of being in which Jesus represented the psychic level that was intermediate between the superior category of the Father and the base level of the material world. He also argued the importance of sacramental rites of initiation derived from early Christian literature.

Origen – a well-respected theologian of the early church – mentions him about fifty times in his commentary on St John: sometimes favourably, sometimes not. Irenaeus and Tertullian, those harsh critics of Gnosticism, hardly mention him at all. Maybe he was too much of a rationalist – as, for example, when he comments on Luke 12: 8. Luke's words were, 'I assure you that whoever confesses in me publicly, the Son of Man will do the same in him before the angels of God', and Heracleon's comment was:

> Men mistake in thinking that the only confession is that made with the voice before magistrates; there is another confession made in the life and conversation, by faith and works corresponding to the faith. The first confession may be made by a hypocrite: and it is one not required of all; there have been many who have never been called on to make it, as for instance Matthew, Philip, Thomas, Levi (Lebbaeus); the other confession must be made by all. He who has first confessed in his disposition of heart will confess with the voice also when need shall arise and reason require. Well did Christ use, concerning confession, the phrase 'in Me', concerning denial the phrase 'Me'. A man may confess 'Him' with the voice who really denies Him, if he does not confess Him also in action; but those only confess 'in Him' who live in the confession And in corresponding actions.

His point is that one cannot claim to belong to Christ if one has no sense of the Christ within. Gnostics are aware of the spirit within as a motivating force which is impossible to deny. Without that motivating force it is possible to deny the external form of Christ. He goes on to say:

> Nay it is He Whom they embrace and Who dwells in them Who makes confession 'in them'; for He cannot deny Himself. But concerning denial, He did not say whosoever shall deny 'in Me', but whoever shall deny 'Me'; for no-one that is 'in Him' can deny Him. And the words 'before men' do not mean before unbelievers only, but before Christians and unbelievers alike; before the one by their life and conversation, before the others in words.

Here Heracleon is suggesting that one might preach to the unconverted, but that one can only bear witness by living one's faith.

However it was Ptolemaeus who seemed to have been the disciplined thinker, able to bring consistency to the contradictions in the various Gnostic dogmas espoused by Valentinus. It is he who provided rules for interpreting Mosaic law and his *Epistle to Flora* (one of his disciples), which was probably written towards the end of the second century AD, quotes sayings from Jesus and relates them to other sources.

Basilides

Basilides by comparison was an ascetic. He only reluctantly permitted marriage on the grounds that it is better to marry than to burn. To Basilides, the passions were an unnatural accumulation which encrusted the spiritual essence, due to the latter's entanglement in the physical realm; sin consisted of a preoccupation with materiality and salvation involved the disentanglement of spirit from matter.

According to third-century Eusebius, the first significant Christian historian:

> There proceeded a power with, as it were, the double jaws and twin heads of a serpent, which produced the authors of two different heresies . . . Satorninus, an Antiochene in Syria, and Basilides, an Alexandrian in Egypt.

Basilides considered that suffering was not something to be escaped but that, through ascetism and faith, it was a blessing, designed to turn the spiritual essence away from its entanglement in matter.

Irenaeus was, as ever, scathing about the followers of Basilides, claiming that they:

> By living lewder lives than the most uncontrolled heathen, they brought blasphemy upon his name.

Basilides rejected the orthodox Christian idea of the resurrection of the flesh – he taught that only souls are saved, for bodies are worth nothing. This may be the source of Irenaeus' accusation, even though Basilides himself taught ascetism. He also taught that all suffering was the result of sin – and evil was the outcome of the actions of Jahweh (Jehovah). True Christians would reject the Old Testament as he did and the crucified Jesus was, for him, a symbol of materialistic worship: as was the sign of the Cross. The spirit of Christ was valid, as was the allegory of scripture as expressed by the poet Homer and the apostle Paul – from whom, by some accounts, he had received secret revelations. You would therefore only be intellectually acceptable to Basilides if you had mastered the Greek language, and with it Greek philosophy and poetry, as well as the Jewish and Christian scholarship of the time. Only then would you be allowed the self-aware sexual freedom of the elite.

The belief system of Basilides also included a well-developed theory of the final days of the Universe. Once the process of the restoration of the spirit to its natural place within the Pleroma (Fullness) has been accomplished, the Great Primeval Ignorance will spread over all creation. The knowledge of the transcendent realm will be withdrawn forever. Everything will be established in its proper place in the Universe and will continue to exist; but it will act in perfect harmony, free from all desire for anything which is contrary to its nature. This is similar to the Buddhist idea that the Boddhisatvas (sacred souls) will incarnate again and again until everything is returned to its Source.

The Panarion or medicine chest

Epiphanius, Bishop of Salamis, in AD 374–377, formulated the Panarion or 'Medicine chest' – which was a stock of 'Remedies' to offset the so-called poisons of heresy. This work is divided into three books, comprising in all seven volumes, that deal with eighty heresies – not all of them Gnostic. The first twenty heresies are prior to the time of Jesus and the remaining sixty deal with Christian doctrine.

Epiphanius claimed to have secretly joined a Gnostic sect, subsequently reporting on its practices which, he claimed, included the sharing of women in sex orgies. These rites included the practice of *coitus interruptus*, when semen was collected and offered to the Lord as the body of Christ, as well as the consumption of menstrual blood. This, interestingly, has overtones of some of the fertility rites practised by pagans.

Apparently this particular sect even believed that Jesus taught these practices, and that he probably took Mary Magdalene to a mountain, removed a woman from his side, had sex with her and then drank his own sperm. (With the knowledge we have today, this sounds very much like a crude variation of the creation myths.) It seems that the life of a voyeur ultimately did not appeal to Epiphanius. He prayed, resisted and ultimately reported the members of the sect to the bishops. Eighty of them were driven away, leaving only the writings of Epiphanius as a record. In his reports, which deliberately set out to shock, it is possible to see the sect's basic attempts to fuse pagan beliefs with only half-understood spiritual teachings, which makes its Gnostic status questionable.

Despite his antagonism, Epiphanius quotes from the Gospel of Eve in the *Panarion*, a text now lost, which shows Gnostic thought:

> I stood upon a high mountain and saw a tall man, and another of short stature, and heard something like the sound of thunder and went nearer in order to hear. Then he spoke to me and said: I am thou and thou art I, and wherever thou art, there am I and I am sown in all things; and whence thou wilt, thou gatherest me, but when thou gatherest me, then gatherest thou thyself.

However the following quote shows Epiphanius' lack of understanding of the Gnostic concept that there is a part of the Divine in everything:

> They say that the same soul is scattered about in animals, beasts, fish, snakes, humans, trees, and products of nature.

In a further reference to ancient pagan fertility rites, semen was ritually spilt on the ground as an offering to Mother Earth in order to ensure bountiful crops. We must therefore make the assumption that the following ritual was simply a transfer of those rites to 'the body of Christ':

> And the pitiful pair, having made love, then proceed to hold up their blasphemy to heaven, the woman and the man

> taking the secretion from the male into their own hands and standing looking up to heaven. They hold the impurity in their hands and pray . . . and say 'We offer you this gift, the body of Christ'. And then they consume it, partaking of their shamefulness, and they say: 'This is the body of Christ and this is the Pasch for which our bodies suffer' . . . When they fall into a frenzy among themselves, they soil their hands with the shame of their secretion, and rising, with defiled hands pray stark naked, as if through such an action they were able to find a hearing with God.

Early Gnostics thought that the power of the soul was to be found in sexual body fluids, semen and menses. Allowing semen to beget children in this world would play into the hands of the evil archon or intermediary god, so the sect would abort the foetus if a woman became pregnant by accident, thus making this entrapment impossible. This practice is diametrically opposed to the Valentinian idea that sex was to be used to bring spiritual awareness into the world. One cannot help but feel that Epiphanius deliberately sets out to shock his readers:

> If one of them fails to anticipate the emission of the seed from the natural effluence and the woman becomes pregnant, then listen to something even more dreadful which they dare to do. Extracting the foetus at whatever time they choose to do the operation, they take the aborted infant and pound it up in a mortar with a pestle, and mixing in honey and pepper and some other spices and sweet oils so as not to become nauseous, all the members of that herd of swine and dogs gather together and each partakes with his finger of the crushed-up child.

Before moving too far away from the time when Jesus was actually alive on this earth, we should look at the life of Simon Magus (the Magician or master).

Simon Magus

Simon Magus is thought to be either a complete charlatan or one of the founding fathers of Gnosticism. He is only once mentioned in the Bible, so anything else that is known about him is probably either pure conjecture, because most surviving reports are by his vitriolic enemies, or else it is part of the legend that has grown up around him. He is said to have been the first Christian heretic. Irenaeus clearly defines his teaching:

> He was worshipped by many as a god, and seemed to himself to be one; for among the Jews he appeared as the Son [thus identifying himself with Jesus], in Samaria as the Father, and among other peoples as the Holy Ghost

Simon Magus obviously attracted a great deal of interest and opprobrium from such critics of Christianity as Hippolytus (d. AD 236), who writes about him in his fifth book in the *Refutation of Heresies* series:

> It seems, then, expedient likewise to explain now the opinions of Simon, a native of Gitta, a village of Samaria; and we shall also prove that his successors, taking a starting point from him, have endeavoured (to establish) similar opinions under a change of name. This Simon being an adept in sorceries, both making a mockery of many . . . and partly also by the assistance of demons perpetrating his villainy, attempted to deify himself. (But) the man was a (mere) cheat, and full of folly, and the Apostles reproved him in the Acts.

Simon's teaching therefore would seem to be as old as, if not older than, St Paul's since Justin (AD 100–167) states in his *Apologia* that Simon worked and taught in Samaria at the time of the emperor Claudius (AD 41–54).

Church historian Eusebius (c260–c341) later approaches Simon by quoting the words of Justin, whom he holds to be 'one of our distinguished writers who lived not long after the time of the apostles':

> And after the ascension of the Lord into heaven the demons put forward certain men who said they were gods, and were not only allowed by you to go unpersecuted, but were even deemed worthy of honours. One of them was Simon, a Samaritan of the village of Gitto, who in the reign of Claudius Caesar performed in your imperial city some mighty acts of magic by the art of demons operating in him, and was considered a god, and as a god was honoured by you with a statue, which was erected in the river Tiber, between the two bridges, and bore this inscription in the Latin tongue, Simoni Deo Sancto, that is, To Simon the Holy God.

This 'fact' has actually proved to be untrue, the statue being to one of Sabine Gods, Semo Sancus.

The Struggle for Spiritual Supremacy

Simon met St Peter (Simon called Peter) when the apostle visited Samaria with St John. A struggle for spiritual supremacy began that only ended in Rome some years later. Simon Magus had attempted to buy the magical skills of the Holy Ghost, so the enmity between himself and Peter was quite considerable. The purchase of religious favour later came to be called simony. Irenaeus, that scourge of Gnostics, tells the tale, which is first recounted in Acts 8: 9–11, 18–20:

> . . . there was a man named Simon who had previously practised magic in the city and amazed the nation of Samaria saying that he himself was somebody great. They all gave heed to him, from the least to the greatest, saying, 'This man is that power of God which is called Great'. And they gave heed to him, because for a long time he had amazed them with his magic. Now when Simon saw that the Spirit was given through the laying on of the apostles hands, he offered them money, saying, 'Give me also this power, that any one on whom I lay my hands may receive the Holy Spirit'. But Peter said to him, 'Your silver perish with you, because you thought you could obtain the gift of God with money'.

There is also a story that Simon, in his search for fame, became friendly with the Emperor Nero, who was fascinated by magic and magicians. Apparently, a competition was set up between Simon Magus and St Peter in an attempt to find out which one was the better able to bring back to life one of Nero's recently dead young relatives. Failure was to be punished by death.

There had already been animosity between Simon Magus and St Peter when the latter proposed to Nero that Simon Magus should read his thoughts. Nero is said to have responded, 'Do you mean me to believe that Simon does not know these things, who both raised a dead man, and presented himself on the third day after he had been beheaded, and who has done whatever he said he would do?' – to which Peter replied, with a touch of self-assurance verging on arrogance: 'But he did not do it before me'.

Later, a furious Simon raged: 'Let great dogs come forth and eat him up before Caesar', at which great dogs suddenly appeared and rushed at Peter. While Peter began to pray he showed the dogs a loaf which he had blessed, whereupon the dogs disappeared. Then Peter said to

Nero: 'Behold, I have shown thee that I knew what Simon was thinking of, not by words but by deeds; for he, having promised that he would bring angels against me, has brought dogs, in order that he might show that he had not god-like but dog-like angels'.

Given that Peter had divine powers, it is not surprising that Simon only produced the illusion of life in the contest involving Nero's dead relative, whereas Peter created the reality. He was able to make the youth stand, walk, talk and eat by calling on the powers of God. This is truly a contest between thaumaturgy and theurgy.

In an attempt to recover his reputation, it is said that Simon vowed that on a certain day he would fly to heaven. He put on some home-made wings and threw himself from a high rock. He soared and flew a short distance but then plummeted when the wings failed, badly injuring himself. He died shortly afterwards and was buried, some say, in a grave dug by himself, having vowed to resurrect himself on the third day. This was an act that Nero believed actually happened, although others suggest that he actually died peacefully in his bed at Antioch.

To be fair to Simon Magus, he was capable of being profound, if somewhat adversarial, as this simulated debate with St Peter shows:

> We have no need of your peace; for if there be peace we shall not be able to make any advance towards the discovery of truth. For robbers and debauchees have peace among themselves, and every wickedness agrees with itself; have met with this view, that for the sake of peace we should give assent to all shall confer no benefit upon the hearers; but on the contrary, we shall impose upon our dear friends. Wherefore do not invoke peace, but rather battle, which is peace; and if you can, exterminate errors. And do not seek for friendship obtained by admissions; for this I would have you know,

> above all, that when two fight with each other, there will be peace when one has been defeated and has fallen.

To which Peter is said to have replied with equal vigour:

> Hear with all attention, O men, what we say. Let us know that the world is a great plain, and that from two states, whose kings are at variance with each other, and whose generals were sent to fight: and suppose the general of the good king gave this command that the armies should without bloodshed submit to the authority of the better king, where they will be safe without danger; but that the opposite general should say, No, but we must fight not to see who is worthy, but who is stronger, may reign, with those who shall escape; which would you rather choose? I doubt not that you would give your hands to the bequeather of the safety of all. And I do not now wish, as Simon says that I do, that assent should be given for the sake of peace, to those things that are spoken amiss, but that truth be sought and order.

Some of Simon's ideas about Gnostic dogma ran contrary to the orthodox belief, although he was baptized into the Christian church. He was, however, able to make those ideas understandable. He maintained that:

- Fire is the first principle
- Fire is bisexual with the male element hidden and the female element called Silence
- The cosmos originated by way of Silence through six aspects of Fire called Roots or Powers in three male-female polarities:
    - Nous (mind) also called Dynamis (power) and Ennoia (thought)

Phone (voice), Onoma (name)
Logismos (reason) and Enthymesis (plan)

- Nous and Ennoia formed an infinite Middle Space, and Ennoia called the image of Nous Father, who is also male and female, and is sometimes called Mother-Father. This androgynous image is present in six Aeons:

  Ouranos (heaven)
  Ge (earth)
  Helios (sun)
  Selene (moon)
  Aer (air)
  Hydor (water)

For sheer showmanship, Simon Magus outstrips any of the Early Gnostics we have seen so far. However, he did live his life according to his own beliefs, not least in his choice of companion, Helena. St Justin has this to say:

> And nearly all the Samaritans and a few even of other nations confess and worship him as the first God. And there went around with at that time a certain Helena who had formerly been a prostitute in Tyre of Phoenicia, and her they call the first idea that proceeded from him.

Simon and Helena

How Simon came by Helena and her place in his scheme of things is a revelation of the way in which dogma and lifestyle can overlap; and arrogance and misapprehension can be strange bedfellows.

Claiming to be a redeemer when teaching in Tyre, he found Helena working as a prostitute on the roof of a brothel and recruited her as a manifestation of Ennoia (First Thought). He reasoned that she was the Lost Sheep forced by angels to wander through centuries of incarnations, including the body of Helen of Troy, until she landed up in the brothel to be redeemed by him. He then purchased her to be his constant companion. The assumption has to be that he thought he was emulating Jesus, thus perhaps lending weight to the idea that Mary Magdalene was a special companion to Jesus, as we see later.

That Simon's version of creation had staying power is illustrated by the fact that Simonian churches continued until the era of Constantine – mostly in Syria, Phrygia, Egypt and Rome. Two schools of thought developed. The Syrian school emphasized libertinism, magic and a pagan worship of Simon and Helena as gods while the Egyptian school was more staid and prosaic, being dedicated to philosophy. It is this branch which is said to have influenced Menander and Satornilos.

Every magician has an assistant who often takes over the role of leader, and Simon's assistant was Menander.

Menander and Satornilos

Menander regarded Simon as an incarnation of Nous, the Great Power of God. He accepted that this Boundless Power, beholding the crimes of the angels, had descended into the lower regions where Simon appeared as a man. He believed that Simon had revealed himself as Father to the Samaritans (non-orthodox Jews, one of the ten tribes of Israel, who kept the Law but rejected the rest of the Bible) and as the Son to the Jews.

As the Son, he suffered a docetic crucifixion and resurrection. As a man, he offered salvation to his fellow Simonians through his divine knowledge – in other words, knowledge of the male-female Mother-Father. Menander did not see the necessity for countless reincarnations. His teaching was that if you were baptized into his particular group you would not 'die' but would receive everlasting life. He does seem to have understood the basic principles of Simon's belief in himself as redeemer, and to have personalized him as an aspect of God.

In contrast, Satornilos (or Satorninus) believed himself to be an angel. He thought that Jesus came to Earth to destroy Jehovah, or the evil powers, and to rescue all who have the divine spark within them. Satornilos taught that the body of man was formed by inferior angels or builders, but that the Power above sent forth the divine spark into man.

There is a distinct similarity to the doctrines of Paul in Satornilos' teaching, especially with regard to the existence of powers of good and evil. He also believed that sex, marriage and procreation were sinful and came from Satan. Satornilos was, above anything else, an ascetic Gnostic and he is perhaps difficult to understand.

Before we move on to some of the other Gnostic sects that arose at around that time it is worth creating a summary of the exact nature of the basic Simonian teachings that were so much a part of the beginning of Christian Gnosticism:

1. The concept of God as male and female: thus androgynous.
2. The concept of angels, hierarchies and divine emanations.
3. The descent of the soul from heaven, its entrapment and subsequent reincarnations.
4. The existence of tyrannical angels or powers.
5. The concept of an infinite power within man – the universal root – which exists as a potential in all men.

It is well-known that charismatic leaders often give rise to differing schools of thought within their own systems of belief. These differences either depend on how free-thinking they themselves are or how much freedom of thought their followers are allowed.

Chapter Five:

The Personalities of Gnosticism

Even from today's perspective it is difficult to differentiate between miracle and magic and it must have been even more difficult for the simpler people of the early Christian era. While we have the benefit of later knowledge, it would have been difficult for them to differentiate between 'wondrous acts' and acts of wonder (thaumaturgy and theurgy).

Carpocrates

Magic and sorcery are once again evident with Carpocrates who invoked the aid of demons and argued that fornication was not wrong. Plainly taking Iranaeus as his source, Eusebius writes of Carpocrates and his followers in his *Church History Book IV,* thereby perpetuating the myths of their wrongdoings:

> Irenaeus also writes that Carpocrates was a contemporary of these men, [i.e Basilides and his disciples] and that he was the father of another heresy, called the heresy of the Gnostics, who did not wish to transmit any longer the magic arts of Simon, as that one had done, in secret, but openly. For they boasted – as of something great – of love

> potions that were carefully prepared by them, and of certain demons that sent them dreams and lent them their protection, and of other similar agencies; and in accordance with these things they taught that it was necessary for those who wished to enter fully into their mysteries, or rather into their abominations, to practice all the worst kinds of wickedness, on the ground that they could escape the cosmic powers, as they called them, in no other way than by discharging their obligations to them all by infamous conduct.

We cannot help but wonder, first of all, if the phrase the 'heresy of the Gnostics' means Gnosticism as a heresy of the Christians or whether it actually suggests that the Carpocratians were a heretical sect within Gnosticism! Clement of Alexandria is more forthcoming about their infamous conduct, though he does report it as hearsay:

> These then are the doctrines of the excellent Carpocratians. These, so they say, and certain other enthusiasts for the same wickednesses, gather together for feasts (I would not call their meeting an Agape), men and women together. After they have sated their appetites ('on repletion Cypris, the goddess of love, enters', as it is said), then they overturn the lamps and so extinguish the light that the shame of their adulterous 'righteousness' is hidden, and they have intercourse where they will and with whom they will. After they have practiced community of use in this love-feast, they demand by daylight of whatever women they wish that they will be obedient to the law of Carpocrates – it would not be right to say the law of God.

When we look back at the Dionysian rites in Chapter Two it can be seen that there are distinct similarities within them to what is described above.

Theologically, Carpocrates claimed that we are all imprisoned in a cycle of reincarnations by wicked angels, but we will eventually be saved. In order to leave this world, the soul has to pass through every possible condition of earthly life, or it cannot free itself from the material powers. This view is very similar to that of Buddhism.

Carpocrates taught that Jesus was given special powers which enabled him to escape from the thrall of the world's evil spirits and finally ascend to the Father. They went on to say that any soul can achieve the same thing provided it rises above the world's constraints. This means that all of us could theoretically perform the miracles of Jesus and even more, once we have been through a number of transmigrations and cycles of rebirth, known technically as metempsychosis.

All of this was mostly taught in Alexandria from AD 117–138. The Carpocratians, in around AD 130, also had followers in Rome that were led by a woman called Marcellina. The orthodox members found difficulty with this as they believed that women should not be in a position of spiritual authority. Their reverence was saved for teachers such as Carpocrates himself and also Pythagoras and Plato, to whom they built statues.

One of their texts is the 'secret' *Gospel of Mark*, excerpts of which are preserved in a fragment of a letter from Clement of Alexandria. It was written in Greek and discovered by Morton Smith at the Mar Sarba monastery in Palestine in 1958. After denouncing the Carpocratians for their libertinism, Clement goes on to accuse them of having the 'secret gospel', further indicating that there is a system of initiation in place. He says:

> As for Mark, during Peter's stay in Rome, he wrote an account of the Lord's doings, not however declaring all of

> them, nor yet hinting at secret ones, but selecting what he thought most useful for increasing the faith of those who were being instructed. But when Peter died a martyr, Mark came over to Alexandria, bringing both his own notes and those of Peter, from which he transferred to his former book the things suitable to whatever makes for progress towards knowledge. Thus he composed a more spiritual Gospel for the use of those who were being perfected.

It would seem, therefore, that there was a deliberate decision to have two sets of teachings, one for the higher initiates and one for more ordinary adherents. Also, there were yet other teachings which could only be revealed through intuition, for Clement continues:

> Nevertheless, he yet did not divulge the things not be uttered, nor did he write down the hierophantic teaching of the Lord, but to the stories already written he added yet others and, moreover, brought in certain sayings of which he knew the interpretation would as a mystagogue, lead the hearers into the innermost sanctuary hidden by seven (veils). Thus, on sum, he prearranged matters, neither grudgingly nor incautiously, in my opinion, and dying, he left his composition to the church in Alexandria, where it even yet is most carefully guarded, being read only to those who are being initiated into the great mysteries.

This led Morton Smith to think that Mark had a secret doctrine acquired by the Alexandrian church and the Carpocratians, and that Carpocratian Gnosticism was:

> a Platonising development of the primitive secret doctrine and a practice of Jesus himself.

Smith also comments on the probability that the secret Gospel of Mark originated in Egypt and that it may well have developed from 'an older Aramaic Gospel, a source used also by canonical Mark and by John'.

Marcion

Marcion was a contemporary of the early Christians (c.85–c.160) and was the founder of the Marcionites, a sect which is interesting in that it began as Christian and only later became Gnostic. It was one of the first great Christian heresies to rival Catholic Christianity.

In many ways, Marcion was not a typical Gnostic. He was relatively kind about Jehovah, although he did argue that such a God was unworthy of being the progenitor of Jesus. He went so far as to compare his own sayings with those of Jesus in order to suggest that they were at least worthy opponents.

Born in Sinope, Marcion is thought to have been one of the early Christian bishops – his father, with whom he fell out, was certainly the Bishop of Sinope in Pontus. Marcion taught in Asia Minor and then went to Rome where, in AD 144, he was excommunicated from the church. Shortly after his arrival, he is said to have threatened:

> I will divide your Church and cause within her a division, which will last forever.

He then formed a church of his own, which became extremely widespread and powerful. He taught that there were two gods – one the stern, lawgiving, creator God of the Old Testament, and the other the good, merciful God of the New Testament. He considered the creator God the inferior of the two. Marcion also rejected the real incarnation and childhood of Christ, claiming that he was simply a manifestation of the Father, the good God.

Marcion is generally seen as one of the most important leaders of the Gnostics, although he did not share some of the main premises of other Gnostic sects. He believed in salvation by faith rather than by gnosis; he rejected the Gnostic emanation theory; and he sought truth in his own version of the New Testament. In *The Catholic Encyclopaedia*, it is remarked that:

> However daring and capricious this manipulation of the Gospel text, it is at least a splendid testimony that, in Christian circles of the first half of the second century the Divinity of Christ was a central dogma. To Marcion however Christ was God Manifest not God Incarnate. His Christology is that of the Docetae . . . rejecting the inspired history of the Infancy, in fact, any childhood of Christ at all; Marcion's Saviour is a 'Deus ex machina'.

Marcion also completely rejected the Old Testament, claiming it to be a 'scandal': that is, capable of leading the faithful astray. The pure Pauline Gospel had become corrupted and Marcion suggested that even the Apostles – Peter, James and John – had betrayed their trust. He often spoke of 'false apostles' and let his listeners infer who they were.

Marcion did not hold marriage in high esteem and, according to some scholars, it was his attachment to a young Gnostic called Cerdo that originally led him to be excommunicated by the orthodox. He would only baptize those who were not living in matrimony, or were virgins, widows or eunuchs. Celibacy seems to have been the ideal since it created a state of Grace – this being in keeping with some of Christ's teachings. All were welcome to the church, however, but they could not become members if they were married..

Marcionite churches were established in Rome, Palestine, Egypt, Syria, Arabia and parts of Persia and Anatolia. So popular was their theology, even with the more obvious Gnostic sentiments that they later acquired, that many lasted into the eighth century. Marcionism emphasized asceticism and self discipline and ultimately influenced the developments of Manichaeism, as we shall see shortly. Ultimately there was a sort of reverse takeover, for the latter later absorbed it.

An extract from G.S. Mead's book, *Fragments of a Faith Forgotten*, goes a long way to explain why Marcion is attractive to some modern thinkers about the Old Testament:

> With great acumen he arranged the sayings and doings ascribed to Yahweh by the writers and compilers and editors of the heterogeneous books of the Old Testament collection, in parallel columns, so to say, with the sayings and teachings of the Christ in a series of antitheses which brought out in startling fashion the fact that, though the best of the former might be ascribed to the idea of a just God, they were foreign to the ideal of the Good God preached by the Christ. We know how in these latter days the best minds in the Church have rejected the horrible sayings and doings ascribed to God in some of the Old Testament documents, and we thus see how Marcion formulated a protest which must have already declared itself in the hearts of thousands of the more enlightened of the Christian name.

Mead also says:

> The longest criticism of Marcion's views is to be found in Tertullian's invective Against Marcion, written in 207 and the following years. This has always been regarded by the orthodox as a most brilliant piece of work; but by the light of the conclusions arrived at by the industry of modern criticism, and also to ordinary common sense, it appears but a sorry piece of angry rhetoric. . . . But we can hardly

> expect a dispassionate treatment of a grave problem, which has only in the last few years reached a satisfactory solution in Christendom, from the violent Tertullian whose temper may be gleaned from his angry address to the Marcionites: 'Now then, ye dogs, whom the Apostle puts outside, and who yelp at the God of truth, let us come to your various questions! These are the bones of contention, which ye are perpetually gnawing!'

Mead concluded his section on Marcion with an interesting anecdote:

> The Marcionites have also given us the most ancient dated Christian inscription. It was discovered over the doorway of a house in a Syrian village, and formerly marked the site of a Marcionite meeting house or church, which curiously enough was called a synagogue. The date is October 1, AD 318 and the most remarkable point about it is that the church was dedicated to 'The Lord and Saviour Jesus, the Good' – 'Chrestos' not Christos. In early times there seems to have been much confusion between the two titles. Christos is the Greek for the Hebrew Messiah, Anointed, and was the title used by those who believed that Jesus was the Jewish Messiah. This was denied, not only by the Marcionites, but also by many of their Gnostic predecessors and successors. The title Chrestos was used of one perfected, the holy one, the saint; no doubt in later days the orthodox, who subsequently had the sole editing of the texts, in pure ignorance changed Chrestos into Christos wherever it occurred; so that instead of finding the promise of perfection in the religious history of all the nations, they limited it to the Jewish tradition alone, and struck a fatal blow at the universality of history and doctrine.

If Marcion was an untypical Gnostic, Mani (AD 216–276), belonged more to the second phase of Gnostic thought.

Mani

An attempted breaker of the mould of Gnosticism, Mani was born in Iran, spoke Aramaic and claimed to be a visionary. He first encountered his spiritual Self at the age of twelve and experienced it again at the age of twenty-five. The basis for his entire myth, the encounter with his 'twin' or transcendental Self, is Gnostic, very much in the spirit of Valentinus:

> I recognised him and understood that he was my Self from whom I'd been separated.

This entity instructed him to preach a new religion in words that are said to have come from the Living God:

> I had revealed to me all that has happened, and all that shall happen, everything that the eye sees, and the ear hears, and the thought thinks. Through him I understood everything. Through him I saw everything.

The encounter with one's twin or – in today's terms – the Higher Self is central to the life of every Manichaean. It is the mystery of conjunction, the holy marriage of ego and Self, and it is now a recognized psychological aspect of the journey towards Truth.

From the onset, the new Manichaean religion seems very like the old Gnosticism, which believed in two gods; that the world is evil and matter is tainted; and that only by knowing oneself is it possible to find one's true self. All but the ascetic or elect would have to undergo reincarnation. The elect were those who did not indulge in fornication, procreation, possessions, cultivation, harvesting, meat eating and wine drinking; and who did not need to be born again into a variety of bodies.

The elect lived according to the Sermon on the Mount and there was a lower class of auditors who were allowed to have wives or concubines and to practise birth control. The so-called elect, who were at home with self-denial and other restrictions so that their soul was able to return to Paradise, naturally required others in the cult to help them keep body and soul together with work and money.

Mani considered himself to be one of a line of prophets that included Adam, Buddha, Zoroaster and Jesus. There were converts to Manichaeism in India, China, Turkey, Persia and the Roman Empire and these spawned neo-Manichaean sects, some of which lasted in Bulgaria, Armenia and southern France until at least the tenth century. He wanted to found a universal religion which would iron out the contradictions he claimed existed in all the other religions and eventually replace them with spiritual ideas which were true, good and beautiful.

Keith Hopkins, Cambridge University Professor of Medieval History, tells a story about Mani's arrogance and the celebrity status which is attributed to him. Persian King Bahram I had summoned Mani to court:

> He kept Mani waiting, while he finished his dinner, and then, on his way out to hunt, came into the audience chamber, leaning with one arm on his young daughter-in-law, and with his other arm resting on the severe Zoroastrian High Priest Kartir. The hostile king said to Mani 'You are not welcome'. The Lord (aka Mani) said 'What wrong have I done?' The king said angrily: 'I have sworn not to let you into this country; what are you good for, since you go neither hunting or fighting?' But then he grudgingly conceded that Mani might be useful for curing and healing. Mani surprisingly colluded with this characterisation. The Lord replied: 'I have

> not done you any harm. Always I have done good to your family. Many are the servants of yours I have freed from demons and witches . . . many were at the point of death, but I revived them'. His pleas were of no avail.

Professor Hopkins then makes the point that Mani now plays out the drama of the strange death so often seen in mystery religions and the similarities with the life of Jesus.

> Bahram I ordered Mani's imprisonment and execution, though according to some accounts, Mani simply died in prison, cruelly loaded with chains. His head, or his flayed skin stuffed with hay, was displayed at the city gate. So the emerging myth of Mani's life, now (like Jesus) had its dramatic trial and unjust ending, its hostile priests and martyr's death, which faithful Manichees celebrated annually at the key point of their liturgical calendar in March, and called it a crucifixion.

It is worth noting that the myths of the coming Messiah and the Redeemer were well known at that time. Since the basic idea within Manicheaism is of life being an illusion or a period of forgetting, following is a typically pessimistic Manichean hymn:

> Since I have been bound to the flesh
> I have forgotten my divinity.
> I was forced to drink the cup of madness
> I was forced to turn my hand against myself.
> The Powers and Principalities
> Approached and armed themselves against me . . .
> Be an enchanter of Light
> And lay a spell on them till I pass . . .

The fact that St Augustine (AD 354–430) had been an auditor within the Manichaean church before he became a priest and Father of the Roman Catholic church serves to demonstrate just how fluid the various strands of Christianity were. Dealing with the question of relationships in some of his later writings, his assertion that the reproductive instinct is not part of human nature but something which was inherited after the Fall is very Manichaean.

Bishop Berkeley, an eighteenth century English philosopher who argued that nothing is real but everything is in the mind (a viewpoint known as solipsism), penned the following aphorism:

> Atheism and Manicheism would have few supporters if mankind were in general attentive.

Gnosticism and the Major Monotheisms

During the period in which the New Testament was being written and Christians were trying to apply some coherence to their beliefs, four particular Gnostic beliefs came into prominence:

1. The story of Genesis was reinterpreted showing the Jewish God to be jealous and enslaving; freedom was knowing how to escape from enslavement to that God.
2. There arose a tradition of Jesus' sayings containing hidden wisdom and meaning.
3. The belief in the soul's ascent to union with the divine as a way of salvation was adopted from the popular forms of Platonism.
4. The myth of the descent of a divine being from the heavenly world to reveal that world as the true home of the soul was developed.

These last three traditions lie behind many conflicts or discrepancies in the interpretation of New Testament writings.

Changing Times

At the time that many of the events described in this book were taking place, the Middle East was a ferment of ideas – some complementary, others conflicting: a fertile hotbed for intellectuals with a case to make, an argument to present or an ego to advance. Ideas not only travelled through the local movement of people but also along the trade routes that extended from Asia in the east, Egypt in the southwest and Greece in the north.

By now the Jewish religion had been established as the first monotheism in hundreds of years so it was relatively resistant to outside influences, although it developed its own brand of Gnosticism, as we shall see. Christianity was riddled with logical and theological uncertainties – with the followers of John calling other Christians heretics – before it established an uneasy orthodoxy; hence it was vulnerable to outside influences. Islam was hundreds of years into a future in which it was able to pick and choose what to believe; and polytheistic paganism, which antedated Judaism, was just about surviving in the face of a determined attack by the monotheists.

The situation was different in Greece, of course, where first Pythagoras and then Plato demonstrated their massive intellects by making fundamental contributions to what the twentieth-century philosopher and mathematician A.N. Whitehead called *The Adventures of Ideas*. Incidentally, Whitehead also described modern philosophy as 'a series of footnotes to Plato', thus demonstrating how important the Greek thinker was.

First, then, we must go back to the Greeks. We will start with Pythagoras and his contribution to Gnosticism.

Pythagoras

Pythagoras (580–500 BC) is perhaps best known today for his theorem about right-angled triangles, in which the square on the side of the hypotenuse is equal to the sum of the squares on the other two sides. A major mathematician and philosopher, he believed that everything was based on number. In his own words:

> Number is the ruler of forms and ideas, and is the cause of gods and demons.

.He also expressed the progression from void (the undefined) to form in a very succinct way:

> The principle of all things is the monad or unit; arising from this monad the undefined dyad or two serves as material substratum to the monad, which is cause; from the monad and the undefined dyad spring numbers; from numbers, points; from points, lines; from lines, plane figures; from plane figures, solid figures; from solid figures, sensible bodies, the elements of which are four, fire, water, earth and air.

Within certain variations of Gnosticism (especially those inspired by Monoismus, an Arabian), the higher being that created lesser gods, or elements, was also known as the Monad.

Bertrand Russell, a mathematician and philosopher like Pythagoras, described him as 'one of the most interesting and puzzling men in history. As well as being the discoverer of a large body of mathematics that laid the foundation of much scientific thought today, Pythagoras also developed religious ideas in which the main tenet was the transmigration of souls or rebirth. It is not clear whether he learned this from the Orphites or vice versa.

Just as it can be said that when a crowd gathers there are three classes of stranger, Pythagoras postulated that there are three kinds of men. The lowest kind consists of those who come to buy and sell and the next above them are those who come to compete. The best of all are those who simply come to look on. Accordingly, men may be classified as lovers of wisdom, lovers of honour and lovers of gain. A variation on this idea is later seen in the organization of the Gnostic hierarchy.

Pythagoras classed himself as a top-drawer thinker who was associated with the god Apollo. He thought he could remember earlier incarnations and that, as a result, he knew more than other people. Classed as a mystic, he developed some very strange rules. These were

1. the sinfulness of eating beans
2. not to pick up what has fallen
3. not to touch a white cock
4. not to break bread, and not to eat from a whole loaf
5. not to step over a crossbar
6. not to stir the fire with iron
7. not to pick a garland
8. not to sit on a quart measure
9. not to eat heart
10. not to walk on highways
11. not to let swallows share one's roof

This of course all sounds like the behaviour of a man who has become somewhat obsessive. Pythagoras even went so far as to shout at someone in the street who was beating a dog: 'Stop! Don't hit it. It is the soul of a friend. I knew it when I heard its voice.'

Other 'marvels' attributed to him include taming a savage bear by whispering into its ear; charming an eagle so that it perched on his hand; catching and soothing poisonous snakes; persuading an ox to stop eating beans; and keeping landed fish alive. All of these actions were apparently carried out while undertaking a census, predicting earthquakes, dispelling plagues and storms and calming violent seas.

Nothing as magical as that could be attributed to any modern mathematician.

Pythagoras' influence also extended through Orpheus to the reform of Orphism, (see page 41) which in turn reformed the worship of Dionysus. That influence can be seen reaching far into the future: into Shakespeare's *Twelfth Night*, for instance:

> Clown: What is the opinion of Pythagoras concerning wildfowl?
> Malvolio: That the soul of our grandam might haply inhabit a bird.
> Clown: What thinkest though of his opinion?
> Malvolio: I think nobly of the soul, and no way approve his opinion.
> Clown: Fare thee well; remain thou still in darkness; thou shalt hold the opinion of Pythagoras ere I will allow of thy wits.

Pythagoras also exerted a profound influence on the field of medicine. He also discovered the numerical ratios that determine the harmonic intervals of the musical scale, so linking music and mathematics, studies which continue even today. In the same way, he discovered that there are numerous polarities, such as hot and cold, wet and dry, sharp and sour – he considered it to be the business of the physician to produce a proper 'blend' of these polarities in the human body. Just as Pythagoras drew on the religions of the East for some of his ideas, so many of the findings of the East found their way into the care of the body and later into medicine.

Plato

We have already met Plato, a follower of Pythagoras, in Chapter Three.

Pythagoras and Plato (488–438 BC) come together in Plato's book the *Timaeus*, in which the hero is a Pythagorean. He says, in Bertrand Russell's translation:

> What is unchanging is apprehended by intelligence and reason; what is changing is apprehended by opinion. The world being sensible cannot be eternal, and must have been created by God. Since God is good, He made the world after the pattern of the eternal . . . He wanted everything as like Himself as possible. God desired that everything should be good, and nothing bad, as far as possible . . .

'Thus it appears', Russell continues, 'that Plato's God unlike the Jewish and Christian God, did not create the world out of nothing, but rearranged pre-existing material. He put intelligence in the soul, and the soul in the body.' If this sounds as if God is describing Pythagoras and Plato, then perhaps it is inadvertent and not a massive arrogance on Plato's part.

Like Pythagoras, Plato also believed in reincarnation, but with a caveat that the soul becomes impure as the result of frequent transmigrations. By subscribing to this belief he faces east and takes on an aspect of Hindu and Buddhist *karma (*Sanskrit for 'deed'): *karma* means an individual's physical and mental actions. The actions in one's life determine the consequences of a person's life on earth and during subsequent lives. One must not 'forget' the consequences of any action but must accept responsibility for those actions. All of this reinforces the argument that many of Plato's core ideas can only be understood by living life in a certain way – mindfully – otherwise they become almost incommunicable; just as the Gnostics believed in an intuitive knowledge that could only be acquired by privileged adherents.

When Jewish Scriptures were introduced into Greek intellectual circles they had a huge influence on the development of Platonic thought. The bringing together of the creation narrative of Genesis and the cosmology of Plato's *Timaeus* inaugurated a whole series of explorations of philosophical and cosmological ideas which were finally gathered together in Plotinus' *Enneads.*

Plotinus

Plotinus, who developed Neoplatonism in the third century AD, is said to bridge the intellectual gap between Greece and Christendom. Like any good Gnostic, he eschewed the teachings of science as it then was and encouraged his disciples to 'withdraw into themselves and begin their exploration in the depths of the psyche'. In his *Enneads* he argued that:

> We here, for our part, must put aside all else and be set on This alone, become This alone, stripping off all encumbrances; we must make haste to escape from here, impatient of our earthly bonds, to embrace God with all our being, that there may be no part of us that does not cling to God. There we may see God and ourself as by law revealed; ourself in splendour, filled with the light of Intellect, or rather, light itself, pure, buoyant, aerial, become – in truth, being – a god.

Plotinus' sole concern is with the well-being (*eudaimonia*) of the human soul and the paradox is that although he was influenced by Gnostic ideas, he was a staunch critic of the movement.

Preceding Plotinus were the so-called Chaldean Oracles which contained, according to the *Encyclopaedia Britannica* (2001), 'a hodgepodge of Popular Greek religious philosophy'. Plotinus took what was best from them, in his eyes, and fitted the ideas in with his own brand of Platonism. He accounted for the materialization of an inferior and defective cosmos from the perfect mind of the divinity by saying that all objective existence is simply an external expression of a deity which is essentially contemplative. The core belief of Neoplatonists seems to be in:

> a plurality of levels of being, arranged in hierarchical descending order, the last and lowest comprising the physical universe, which exists in time and space and is perceptible to the senses.

The other end of the spectrum is, therefore, as quoted in the *Encyclopaedia Britannica* (2001):

> The highest level of being, and through it all of what in any sense exists, derives from the ultimate principle, which is absolutely free from determinations and limitations and utterly transcends any conceivable reality, so that it may be said to be beyond being.

Bertrand Russell reports on a discussion of the Gnostic view and says that Plotinus admits that some parts of Gnostic doctrine, such as the hatred of matter, may be due to Plato, but holds that the other parts, which do not come from Plato, are untrue. Russell is quite explicit and pays homage to Plotinus' view that the heavenly bodies are beautiful:

> His objections to Gnosticism are of two sorts. On the one hand, he says that Soul, when it creates the material world, does so from memory of the divine, and not because it is fallen; the world of sense, he thinks, is as good as a sensible world can be . . . There is another reason for rejecting the Gnostic point of view. The Gnostics think that nothing

> divine is associated with the sun, moon and stars; they were created by an evil spirit. Only the Soul of man, among things perceived, has any goodness. But Plotinus is firmly persuaded that the heavenly bodies are the bodies of god-like beings, immeasurably superior to man. According to the Gnostics, 'their own soul, the soul of the least of mankind, they declare deathless, divine; but the entire heavens and the stars within the heavens have had no communion with the Immortal Principle, though these are far purer and lovelier than their own souls'.

Russell makes the point that Plotinus sees the world as it is very clearly and does not subscribe to the view that the world is evil or ugly:

> For the view of Plotinus there is authority in the Timaeus (Plato), and it was adopted by some Christian Fathers, for instance, Origen . . . There is in the mysticism of Plotinus nothing morose or hostile to beauty. But he is the last religious teacher for many centuries of whom this can be said. Beauty, and all the pleasures associated with it, came to be thought to be of the Devil; pagans as well as Christians came to glorify ugliness and dirt. Julian the Apostate, like contemporary orthodox saints, boasted of the populousness of his beard. Of all this, there is nothing in Plotinus.

Plotinus, in brief, castigated the Gnostics for 'thinking very well of themselves, and very ill of the universe'.

Christian Innovation

As recently as 1979, some theologians were still having arguments as to whether or not this viewpoint influenced Christianity in any obvious way. Two opinions are worth quoting. J.S. Spong says:

> When Christianity severed itself from Judaism the Christian faith itself became distorted.

The *Harvard Theological Review* (1959) noted:

> The most important fact in the history of Christian doctrine was that the father of Christian theology, Origen, was a Platonic philosopher at the school of Alexandria. He built into Christian doctrine the whole cosmic drama of the soul, which he took from Plato . . .

Some of the consequences of these influences are claimed to be a false idea of the messiah and an equally suspect idea that Christians go to heaven at death by surviving as a disembodied soul. Perhaps Origen is better known for having himself castrated because, he explained, Jesus had said that it would advance the Kingdom of Heaven. His reasons were an interpretation of Matthew 19 verse 12.

Origen was an innovator at a time when such an action for Christians could be downright dangerous. He drew extensively upon pagan philosophy in an effort to clarify the Christian faith in a way that was acceptable to scholars, and he succeeded in converting many gifted pagan students of philosophy to his faith. The main Christian movement originally seems to have been Gnostic (based on knowledge) but its followers kept their inner mysteries secret, revealing them only to those who had been initiated into the faith.

Origen did not embrace the dualism of Gnosticism, but instead he took literalist Christianity to a higher level, finding in it a basis for the perfection of the mind, which in his view is what all souls are in their pure form. He was also a great humanist, who believed that all creatures will eventually achieve salvation, including the devil himself.

Much of Origen's teaching shares similarities with that of Valentinus. Origen teaches that the spirits fall away from God and become souls, the world purifies the soul and, more importantly, Jesus brings not just redemption to the faithful but knowledge to those who diligently seek it. The crucial component in Origen's teaching is the operation of free will – through this can be achieved complete consciousness.

The Docetists have also had a widespread influence on Christianity (see page 196): they believed that Jesus was only a man; that the Son of God did not die on the cross; and that the figure was a phantom. The argument is that the Son of God entered this man at baptism and left him on crucifixion:

> And Jesus cried with a loud voice and gave up the ghost.
> (Mark 15: 37)

Interestingly, each of the gospels in the King James Bible says that 'he gave up the ghost', suggesting something somewhat different to an ordinary death. The despair of the cry 'My God, my God, why hast thou forsaken me' has always caused Christian theologians some intellectual anguish because of there seems to be a distinct lack in divine purpose. Jesus' words were 'E-li E-li, la-ma sa-bach-tha-ni?' One translation of the words 'E-li E-li' is said by some to mean 'My power. My power' which would suggest that Jesus experienced this inner energy as a separate force within himself.

Islam

The prophet Mohammed, however, took all of the crucifixion at its face value and was not concerned by the presumption that Jesus died in a less than perfect state ('Be thou perfect as I am perfect' – Genesis 17: 1). Mohammed always recognized Jesus as a prophet like himself –

no more divine than he. Perhaps he was playing safe or else he entertained the pious hope, as Bertrand Russell puts it, that 'prophets should not come to a bad end'. The belief that the figure that hung on the cross was only a phantom remains part of Islamic belief today.

In Southern Iraq, several groups of Islamic Gnostics were known to be in existence by the ninth century. Several other Gnostic sects found refuge there during late antiquity and the Mandaeans continue to live in Southern Iraq. The best-known Islamic Gnostic sect, the Isma-illiyah, of which the Aga Khan is the religious leader, also still practise there.

It is interesting to note that some of the mythological themes that are central to the Gnostic religion are distinctly similar, in Islamic terms, to the *Apocryphon of St John*. These are:

- The cycles of the seven prophets
- The throne and the letters
- Kuni, the creative principle, who is feminine
- The higher Pentad; four senses plus spirit
- The infatuation of the lower demiurge
- The seven planets and the twelve signs of the zodiac
- The existence of a divine Adam
- The fall and ascent of the soul

When we begin to reach below the surface there is, as always, a consistency in the stories that are attached to different religions, which leads one to believe that there must have been a common source.

Mandeans

The name actually comes from the Aramaic word for knowledge and the Mandaeans are perhaps the last truly Jewish Gnostics in the world. Their culture still shows evidence of their Jewish origin and they revere John the Baptist as a sacred person. However, Jesus is sometimes subservient and is even seen as being evil.

Today, some 15,000 Mandaeans live in Iraq and Iran, attempting to exist peaceably and practice their own beliefs. One of the central points of their religion is baptism in streaming water, which is experienced by every believer several times a year. The Mandean sanctuary, *Mandi*, is a very simple, small house with a slanting roof. In front of this is a pool for baptism which is connected to a nearby river which they call 'Jordan', presumably in commemoration of John the Baptist who baptized his followers in the real River Jordan. The whole area is surrounded by a high fence or wall. Baptisms are performed on Sundays and Mandean baptism can be compared to the Christian communion and the Muslim prayer, *salat.*

Another important ceremony is the funerary mass. When a Mandaean dies a priest performs a complicated rite in order to return the soul to its heavenly abode, where it will receive a spiritual body. In this way, it is believed, the deceased person is integrated into the so-called Secret Adam, the Glory, the divine body of God. This name lends substance to the idea that, along with the *anthropos* (male human) of Poimandres and the Adam Qadmon of later Jewish mysticism, this divine and heavenly figure is ultimately derived from the vision of the prophet Ezekiel (Ezekiel 1: 26). In Mandaean lore, Sophia appears in a degraded form as a mean and lewd creature called the Holy Spirit.

It is unfortunate that even today the Mandeans find themselves persecuted for their beliefs. They are accused of being 'star-worshippers,' a practice that carries the death penalty in a Muslim country, so survival cannot have been easy for them when they have always relied on astrology and working with the correct energy as a way of structuring their lives. Instances of heavy questioning about their political affiliation have also resulted in some distress, particularly as their only desire is to be left alone to practise their own religion in the way that they have done for centuries.

Repression of Gnostics

Early Gnostic writings show that the tendency to isolate Gnostics and repress anyone who did not conform has always been in existence. In the *Testimony of Truth,* which was apparently written in third-century Alexandria, the author attacks other non-ascetic Gnostic sects as heretics, although he does say that the true teacher avoids disputes and makes himself equal to everyone.

During the third period of the interaction between Gnosticism and Christianity – that is, from the end of the second century to the fourth century (see Chapter Four) – there was a significant shift within gnosticism. In some ways it went back to its roots, for it became increasingly de-Christianised as it began to associate itself more with the esoteric, hermetic and non-Christian elements within the existent traditions.

There was also something of a division within Gnosticism itself. Its more ascetic adherents joined the monks in the Egyptian desert, with their combination of Origenist mysticism and asceticism, while those less spiritually inclined sought out those Manichaean or Mandean circles in which they could practise their thaumaturgy.

Gnosticism has always experienced a particular difficulty. Firstly, information must be hidden from those not of like minds; and secondly, the various aspects of knowledge associated with each level of initiation must also be hidden until such time as the initiate is ready to have it revealed. Much information was lost for centuries and it could well have been thought that the Gnostic belief was buried for ever. However, things were changed by a chance find in Egypt.

Chapter Six:

Gnostic Texts

The discovery in Egypt of what has now become known as the Nag Hammadi Library has been the saving grace of Gnosticism – perhaps even preventing its extinction. This immeasurably important discovery included texts once thought to have been entirely destroyed during the struggle to define Christian orthodoxy (literally 'straight thinking').

Nag Hammadi Texts

It is very difficult to avoid the sneaking feeling that only those who were concerned about Gnosticism to the point of paranoia would offer such vehement opposition.

However that may be, it was not until 1945 that Gnosticism once again began to speak up for itself. When two brothers were digging for nitrate (a natural fertilizer) near the northern Egyptian village of Nag Hammadi, they discovered a large clay jar. They had to make up their minds whether the jar contained an evil spirit, in which case they were reluctant to open it, or a 'crock of gold'. Being more venal than fearful, they chipped the lid away but, instead of gold, they found a library of rare and valuable Gnostic texts. Unaware of the real worth of the texts, they are said to have kept the papyri close to their fire, perhaps even burning some of them.

Forty-one of the texts were unknown new works including:

- Gospel of Thomas
- Gospel of Truth
- Treatise on the Resurrection
- Gospel of Philip
- Gospel of Mary
- Wisdom of Jesus Christ
- Revelation of James
- Letter of Peter to Philip
- On the Origin of the World

They were written in Greek during the second and third centuries AD and translated into Coptic (mostly old Egyptian written with Greek lettering) in the fourth century. Some of the texts were Gnostic in origin while others explored Christian themes from a Gnostic point of view. We now know that the Nag Hammadi texts were buried in about AD 365, possibly to avoid destruction during a religious purge. Since their discovery, they have been held in the Coptic Museum in Cairo.

Publication of the texts was first of all delayed by the Anglo-French war against Egypt that followed the nationalization of the Suez Canal in 1956. It was then impeded by the Arab-Israeli war of 1967 and, later, disputes among scholars. The *Gospel of Thomas* was translated into English during the late 1960s and the others were translated during the next ten years.

In the light of an explanation in *Encyclopaedia Britannica* (2001), it is not surprising that the texts represented a jumble of different dogmas between them:

> The doctrine of the soul taught in Gnostic communities was almost identical to that taught in the mysteries: the soul emanated from the Father, fell into the body and had to return to its former home.

The Greeks interpreted the national religions of the Greek Orient chiefly in terms of Plato's philosophical and religious concepts, which included the notion that people were fallen gods so divine forms within them could be reached by reason, and that life on earth was dark and impure. Interpretation in Platonic concepts was also the means by which the Judeo-Christian set of creeds was thoroughly assimilated to Greek ideas by the early Christian thinkers, Clement of Alexandria and Origen.

Gospel of Thomas

We saw three of the verses from the *Gospel of Thomas* in the introduction. Here are some further extracts from the English translation of that text, which indicates whether Jesus is speaking to one person (sg.) or to many (pl.). His disciples ask for guidance and Jesus simplifies his instructions to such an extent that he asks them simply to be honest, since the higher authority, which is heaven, is aware of the motivation:

> 4. Jesus said, 'The man old in days will not hesitate to ask a small child seven days old about the place of life, and he will live. For many who are first will become last, and they will become one and the same.'
>
> 5. Jesus said, 'Recognize what is in your (sg.) sight, and that which is hidden from you (sg.) will become plain to you (sg.). For there is nothing hidden which will not become manifest.'
>
> 6. His disciples questioned him and said to him, 'Do you want us to fast? How shall we pray? Shall we give alms? What diet shall we observe?' Jesus said, 'Do not tell lies, and do not do what you hate, for all things are plain in the sight of heaven. For nothing hidden will not become

> manifest, and nothing covered will remain without being uncovered.'

In the next section it is indicated that everything is allotted its proper place in the universe:

> 7. Jesus said, 'Blessed is the lion which becomes man when consumed by man; and cursed is the man whom the lion consumes, and the lion becomes man.'
>
> 8. And he said, 'The man is like a wise fisherman who cast his net into the sea and drew it up from the sea full of small fish. Among them the wise fisherman found a fine large fish. He threw all the small fish back into the sea and chose the large fish without difficulty. Whoever has ears to hear, let him hear.'

At this point is recorded one of the parables which Jesus used in his ministry. It is interesting since it is recorded as Thomas heard it, and not in a standardized version.

> 9. Jesus said, 'Now the sower went out, took a handful (of seeds),and scattered them. Some fell on the road; the birds came and gathered them up. Others fell on rock, did not take root in the soil, and did not produce ears. And others fell on thorns; they choked the seed(s) and worms ate them. And others fell on the good soil and it produced good fruit: it bore sixty per measure and a hundred and twenty per measure.'

Here, Jesus is asking his disciples to think for themselves. He seems to be using fire and light with a slightly more esoteric symbolic meaning than normal and he also puts into words the somewhat nihilistic idea that the heavens will pass away. Also, there is a hint of the idea that there is no real separation:

> 10. Jesus said, 'I have cast fire upon the world, and see, I am guarding it until it blazes.'
>
> 11. Jesus said, 'This heaven will pass away, and the one above it will pass away. The dead are not alive, and the living will not die. In the days when you consumed what is dead, you made it what is alive. When you come to dwell in the light, what will you do? On the day when you were one you became two. But when you become two, what will you do?'

Once again the disciples ask for guidance, perhaps guarding themselves against the future, perhaps hoping that they will be singled out for notice:

> 12. The disciples said to Jesus, 'We know that you will depart from us. Who is to be our leader?" Jesus said to them, 'Wherever you are, you are to go to James the righteous, for whose sake heaven and earth came into being.'

This next section of the Gospel is of particular interest for it reveals a degree of confusion within Thomas. Jesus acknowledges this, but also recognizes that because Thomas is not seeing him clearly he needs additional information which must, however, be given in secret. Such a method is often used when the information needed is of an esoteric nature. Thomas indicates that the information he has been given is extremely powerful but that not everyone can handle it:

> 13. Jesus said to his disciples, 'Compare me to someone and tell me whom I am like.' Simon Peter said to him, 'You are like a righteous angel.' Matthew said to him, 'You are like a wise philosopher.' Thomas said to him, 'Master, my mouth is wholly incapable of saying whom you are like.' Jesus said, 'I am not your (sg.) master. Because you (sg.) have drunk, you (sg.) have become intoxicated from the bubbling spring which I have measured out.' And he took him and withdrew and told him three things. When Thomas returned to his companions, they asked him, 'What did Jesus say to you?' Thomas said to them, 'If I tell you one of the things which he told me, you will pick up stones and throw them at me; a fire will come out of the stones and burn you up.'

If the following section is taken at face value, it would seem that Jesus is beginning to train his disciples in how they can be 'in the world, but not of it'. He is not advocating the usual conduct of a holy man but he is talking about fitting in and being true to oneself:

> 14. Jesus said to them, 'If you fast, you will give rise to sin for yourselves; and if you pray, you will be condemned; and if you give alms, you will do harm to your spirits. When you go into any land and walk about in the districts, if they receive you, eat what they will set before you, and heal the sick among them. For what goes into your mouth will not defile you, but that which issues from your mouth - it is that which will defile you.'

As the verses continue, the reader can almost feel the increase in the energy and the pace of learning. The reported words of Jesus have a slightly more abstract twist to them and he seems to be pushing his followers to think for themselves. In verse 17 he appears to be saying that he knows certain truths which have not been evident before – surely a very Gnostic statement, if we remember the original meaning of gnosis, which is knowledge of the Divine. Verses 18 and 19 have a certain flavour of the Eastern religions about them in their knowledge of totality. Only those initiated into the mysteries would necessarily have a full understanding of these passages.

15. Jesus said, 'When you see one who was not born of woman, prostrate yourselves on your faces and worship him. That one is your father.'

16. Jesus said, 'Men think, perhaps, that it is peace which I have come to cast upon the world. They do not know that it is dissension which I have come to cast upon the earth: fire, sword, and war. For there will be five in a house: three will be against two, and two against three, the father against the son, and the son against the father. And they will stand solitary.'

17. Jesus said, 'I shall give you what no eye has seen and what no ear has heard and what no hand has touched and what has never occurred to the human mind.'

18. The disciples said to Jesus, 'Tell us how our end will be.' Jesus said, 'Have you discovered, then, the beginning, that you look for the end? For where the beginning is, there will the end be. Blessed is he who will take his place in the beginning; he will know the end and will not experience death.'

19. Jesus said, 'Blessed is he who came into being before he came into being. If you become my disciples and listen to

> my words, these stones will minister to you. For there are five trees for you in Paradise which remain undisturbed summer and winter and whose leaves do not fall. Whoever becomes acquainted with them will not experience death.'
>
> 20. The disciples said to Jesus, 'Tell us what the kingdom of heaven is like.' He said to them, 'It is like a mustard seed. It is the smallest of all seeds. But when it falls on tilled soil, it produces a great plant and becomes a shelter for birds of the sky.'

It is perhaps interesting to note that birds were, and indeed often still are, taken as symbols of the soul.

When Jesus speaks in parables, he knows that people will hear him according to their level of understanding (or perhaps initiation). He warns that there will be those who will be in conflict with his followers and who will try to take away what they have. He also seems to suggest that there is a process of regeneration which must take place from a wholly innocent perspective before his followers can become totally aware:

> 21. Mary said to Jesus, 'Whom are your disciples like?' He said, 'They are like children who have settled in a field which is not theirs. When the owners of the field come, they will say, "you expect will (surely) materialize. Let there be among you a man of understanding. When the grain ripened, he came quickly with his sickle in his hand and reaped it. Whoever has ears to hear, let him hear.'
>
> 22. Jesus saw infants being suckled. He said to his disciples, 'These infants being suckled are like those who enter the kingdom.' They said to him, 'Shall we then, as children, enter the kingdom?' Jesus said to them, 'When you make

> the two one, and when you make the inside like the outside and the outside like the inside, and the above like the below, and when you make the male and the female one and the same, so that the male not be male nor the female; and when you fashion eyes in place of an eye, and a hand in place of a hand, and a foot in place of a foot, and a likeness in place of a likeness; then will you enter the kingdom.'

At this point Jesus' disciples recognize that he is on a different plane of existence or, in today's terms, at a different level of consciousness to them. Jesus explains so that they may understand:

> 23. Jesus said, 'I shall choose you, one out of a thousand, and two out of ten thousand, and they shall stand as a single one.'

> 24. His disciples said to him, 'Show us the place where you are, since it is necessary for us to seek it.' He said to them, 'Whoever has ears, let him hear. There is light within a man of light, and he lights up the whole world. If he does not shine, he is darkness.'

In this next part, Thomas gives a version of one of the best-known passages of the Bible and seems to show that while in the world one should observe the world's rules but still remain aloof from everyday concerns:

> 25. Jesus said, 'Love your (sg.) brother like your soul, guard him like the pupil of your eye.'

> 26. Jesus said, 'You (sg.) see the mote in your brother's eye,

> but you do not see the beam in your own eye. When you cast the beam out of your own eye, then you will see clearly to cast the mote from your brother's eye.'
>
> 27. Jesus said, 'If you do not fast as regards the world, you will not find the kingdom. If you do not observe the Sabbath as a Sabbath, you will not see the father.'

Also there is a passage that seems to draw all of the above thoughts into a coherent, more succinct whole. It is very similar to the information that we have shown in the introduction (verses 1–3):

> Jesus said: 'If those who lead you say to you, see, the kingdom is in heaven, then the birds of heaven will go before you. If they say to you, it is in the sea, then the fish will go before you. But the kingdom is within you, and it is outside of you . . . Recognize what is in front of you, and what is hidden from you will be revealed to you, for there is nothing hidden that will not be made manifest' . . . Jesus said: 'I am the light that is above them all. I am the all; the all came forth from me, and the all returned to me. Cleave a piece of wood: I am there. Raise up a stone, and you will find me there . . . If you do not fast to the world, you will not find the Kingdom' . . . His disciples said to him: 'On what day will the repose of the dead come into being, and on what day will the new world come?' He said to them: 'What you await has come, but you do not know it' . . . His disciples said to him: 'On what day will the kingdom come?' (Jesus said) 'It will not come while people watch for it; they will not say: Look here it is, or: Look, there it is; but the kingdom of the father is spread out over the earth, and men do not see it.'

These ideas would have seemed new and innovative to Jesus' contemporaries, laying the foundation for what would become very New Testament in sentiment and language.

The Gospel of Truth

Part of a commentary on *The Gospel of Truth* (now in the Nag Hammadi library) in the *Cambridge Companion to the Bible* (1997) comes right back to the idea that Gnosticism is based on knowledge of the Divine, perhaps applied in a particular way:

> The Gospel of Truth referred to by Irenaeus is an extended discourse in which the themes of inner divine knowledge and freedom from the body and earthly involvement set out in the Gospel of Thomas are developed more freely. The references to the original gospel material found in the New Testament are even fewer than in Thomas and purely metaphorical. Jesus is said to have been nailed to a tree 'because Error was angry at him'; from that situation symbolizing a threat from evil (the cross) Jesus published the edict of the Father which consisted of letters written by Unity. The primary role of Jesus throughout the text is to enlighten those in conceptual darkness, thereby making visible the Invisible Father.
>
> The goal of human existence is to know one's origin and destiny, the latter of which is the attainment of unity by self-purification through knowledge. The parable of the lost sheep is a metaphor for achieving the completeness (pleroma) of being. The Son is the name of the Father and came from the depths of the Father to explain him and to disclose secret things. None of the issues, aims or values of the original tradition – the renewal of the created order, the transformation of the covenant people, God's offer of

> reconciliation to an estranged, disobedient humanity – are evident in this Gnostic document which claims to offer the secret clues to understanding Jesus and his role as renewer of the covenant.

The Nag Hammadi texts confirmed much of what theologians had already deduced from the published works of such critics of Gnosticism as Irenaeus (in the second century) and Tertullian – who later became a Montanist. These men must have had recourse to the original texts and were honourable enough, it is assumed, to quote accurately from them. The main conclusion was that Gnostics were mostly individual believers or members of cliques within Christian congregations. Beyond a set of core beliefs, they had no agreed, universal doctrine and there were many different published versions.

Other Texts

Women often wrote religious texts and they also featured prominently in many writings. Mary Magdalene, for example, was held in particularly high regard, often being second in status to Jesus. She was one of a profusion of Marys, along with the Virgin Mary, mother of Jesus, and Mary of Bethany, Lazarus' sister. Some scholars believe they were all the same person. The Gospels provide no clarification, although Luke (8: 2) does speak of one of Jesus' followers 'who had been healed of evil spirits and infirmities, who was called Mary and came from the town of Magdala, and out of whom Jesus had exorcised seven devils'.

Just before this, Luke recounts that he was having dinner with a Pharisee when an unnamed woman washed Jesus' feet with her tears, dried them with her hair and then anointed them. The act, and Luke's description of it, was seemingly erotic but it was, in fact, an act of veneration and devotion. Matthew and Mark also tell the same tale, but because they set it before the Last Supper their words have more spiritual potency. Whether or not the woman was a separate person or part of a conflation of three Marys, there is no doubt about her significance for feminists of today.

In the *Pistis Sophia,* which is part of an earlier find of texts now known as the Askew Codex, we find passages which give Mary special status:

> Now it happened when Maria finished saying these words, he said : 'Excellent, Maria. Thou art blessed beyond all women upon earth, because thou shalt be the pleroma of all Pleromas and the completion of all completions.' But when Maria heard the Saviour saying these words, she rejoiced greatly and she came before Jesus, she prostrated herself in his presence, she worshipped at his feet, she said to him : 'My Lord, hear me that I question thee on this word before thou speakest with us of the places to which thou hast gone.'
>
> Jesus answered and said to Maria : 'Speak openly and do not fear. I will reveal all things which thou seekest.'

The Askew Codex was bought by the British Museum in 1795, having been previously acquired by a Dr. Askew from an unknown source. It is more commonly known by the name '*Piste Sophiea Cotice*' that is inscribed upon its binding, and it appears to deal with the post-resurrectional period. This was the period in which Jesus remained upon the earth but revealed himself as the Being of Light, conferring Gnosis upon his disciples – both men and women. G.R.S. Mead suggested that a more appropriate name might be '*Books of the Saviour*'. The Supreme Being was often alternatively referred to as either he or she in such texts, thereby recognizing the degree of androgyny that was involved.

The Akhmin Codex containing the *Gospel of Mary* (it was

discovered along with the *Apocryphon of John* and the *Sophia of Jesus Christ* in Cairo in 1896) also antedated the discovery of the Nag Hammadi text by some years. Some pages are missing from the Cairo text but, even so, both these texts were translated and are now in the Nag Hammadi Library in the United States.

An extract follows, that touches in on what is now known as alchemy and the basic laws of nature:

> Will matter then be destroyed or not?
> The Saviour said, All nature, all formations, all creatures exist in and with one another, and they will be resolved again into their own roots.
> For the nature of matter is resolved into the roots of its own nature alone.
> He who has ears to hear, let him hear.

Once again Jesus indicates that those who have the requisite knowledge will understand, as he does in the next section, using the words 'He who has a mind to understand . . .' He also says that there is no sin except that that we create for ourselves:

> Peter said to him, 'Since you have explained everything to us, tell us this also: What is the sin of the world'?
> The Saviour said 'There is no sin, but it is you who make sin when you do the things that are like the nature of adultery, which is called sin.
> That is why Good came into your midst, to the essence of every nature in order to restore it to its root.'
> Then He continued and said, 'That is why you become sick and die, for you are deprived of the one who can heal you.
> He who has a mind to understand, let him understand.'

Jesus appears also to be suggesting that passion is an aspect of the physical realm and not part of the peace that is inherent in nature. Interestingly, this is quite a Taoist thought. The term the Son of Man is used here and it probably refers to the divine man mentioned in Ezekiel (2: 26):

> 'Matter gave birth to a passion that has no equal, which proceeded from something contrary to nature. Then there arises a disturbance in its whole body.
> That is why I said to you Be of good courage, and if you are discouraged be encouraged in the presence of the different forms of nature.
> He who has ears to hear, let him hear.'
> When the Blessed One had said this, He greeted them all saying, 'Peace be with you. Receive my peace unto yourselves.
> Beware that no one lead you astray saying Lo here, lo there! For the Son of Man is within you.
> Follow after Him!
> Those who seek Him will find Him.
> Go then and preach the gospel of the Kingdom.
> Do not lay down any rules beyond what I appointed you, and do not give a law like the lawgiver lest you be constrained by it.'
> When He said this He departed.

It has been discovered from existent texts that some Gnostic groups had birth rituals in which initiates were baptized according to a fourfold ritual:

> In the name of the Father unknown to all
> In the Truth, Mother of all,

> In the One who came down upon Jesus,
> In the union, redemption and communion of powers

In addition, the dead or dying were anointed to ease the progress of the soul beyond the demonic Archons towards the Supreme Being.

Historical Accuracy

To put it succinctly, the Nag Hammadi texts covered a great deal of ground: writings about the Gnostic versions of creation and salvation; observations and commentaries on the nature of reality; the nature of the soul and the relationship of the soul to the world; and a treatise on Gnostic sacramental theology. There were also discussions of the feminine principle, writings on the lives and experiences of some of the apostles, an anthology of the sayings of Jesus and accounts of incidents in his life.

So we must ask if the Nag Hammadi Gnostic texts are historically accurate. Can any Gnostic even today echo the words used by Luke in the New Testament, when he attempted to establish some credibility for the events described there? Luke writes:

> Many have undertaken to draw up an account of the things that have been fulfilled among us, just as they were handed down to us by those who from the first were eye-witnesses and servants of the word. Therefore, since I myself have carefully investigated everything from the beginning, it seemed good also to me to write an orderly account for you, most excellent Theophilus, so that you may know the certainty of the things you have been taught. (Luke 1: 14).

The Gnostic texts are not eye-witness reports so the answer is probably 'No', they were not historically accurate. Also, the linguistic ability of those who translated them from Greek into Coptic is at best variable. Until the fifteenth century, when printing was invented, copies had to be handmade and the accuracy of the transcription could not be guaranteed. There is even doubt that texts that are called gospels are gospels at all in the traditional meaning of the word – that is, the presentation of the life of Jesus in all its variety as preacher, teacher and healer.

It is generally accepted that these texts are not the 'lost books of the Bible'. They do contain special pleading on behalf of Gnostics as in, for example, the Letter of Peter to Philip in which the apostles ask after the resurrection, 'Lord, we would like to know the deficiency of the aeons and of their pleroma'. There are also other accounts which are closer to abstract Gnostic cosmology than the mainstream Christian language of fishermen like Peter and other ordinary working people.

It is true that many of the 114 sayings in the *Gospel of Thomas* might have come from Matthew, Mark and Luke – however they are not presented in a social context which would make them easier to deconstruct. Biblical scholar F.F. Bruce in *Jesus and Christian Origins Outside the New Testament* observes that:

> The sayings of Jesus are best to be understood in the light of the historical circumstances in which they were spoken. Only when we have understood them thus can we safely endeavour to recognise the permanent truth which they convey. When they are detached from their original historical setting and arranged in an anthology, their interpretation is more precarious.

It is important to understand that even in the Bible itself there are many examples in which the sayings of Jesus change with the perceptions and the personality of the reporter. For instance, here is a simple illustration of what happens even when an uncomplicated event is described:

> Thomas says, 'Jesus said, "Why do you wash the outside of the cup? Did you not realise that he who made the inside is the same one who made the outside."' Luke says, 'And the Lord said unto him, "Now you Pharisees cleanse the outside of the cup and the dish, but inside you are full of extortion and wickedness. You fools! Did not he who made the outside make the inside also? So give for alms those things that are within; and see everything will be clean for you."' Matthew is different again with 'Woe to you scribes and Pharisees, hypocrites! For you clean the outside of the cup and of the plate, but inside they are full of greed and self-indulgence. You blind Pharisee! First clean the inside of the cup, so that the outside also may become clean.'

We shall never know which is the right version, but maybe it is of no importance in a biblical world full of metaphor and allegory. The gist is there. In any case, orthodoxy has it that the Bible is about faith not fact. Inconsistency among apologists is seen as a virtue.

Differences in interpretation come from the fact that the orthodox church was trying to clarify, first to itself and later to the world, how it understood the teachings of Christ. The premise of the Gnostic church was not so much the understanding of the teachings, but more the understanding of the links with divinity.

So far as the Nag Hammadi texts are concerned, there is also something of a problem in interpreting what has been lost in the ageing of the manuscripts. James Robinson, editor of *The Nag Hammadi Library* points to:

> . . . physical deterioration of the books themselves which began no doubt before they were buried around 400 AD,

> then advanced steadily while they remained buried, and unfortunately was not completely halted in the period between their discovery in 1945 and their final conservation thirty years later.

Robinson likens the translation of the texts to putting together an incomplete jigsaw puzzle. 'When only a few letters are missing,' he says 'they can often be filled in adequately, but larger holes must simply remain a blank.'

There is no way of allaying doubts about the value of the texts as an addition to, or a corroboration of, the Christian message. All that can be said is that they expound on, and explain, Gnosticism. Except to fundamentalist Gnostics, they can in no way be regarded as an alternative message to the orthodox accounts set out in the New Testament, so committed Christians may refresh their memories and their faith by consulting the Bible.

As Patrick Henry writes in his book *New Direction*:

> While the Nag Hammadi materials have made some corrections to the portrayal of Gnosticism in the anti-Gnostic writings of the church fathers, it is increasingly evident that the fathers did not fabricate their opponents' views; what distortion there is comes from selection, not from invention. It is still legitimate to use materials from the writings of the fathers to characterise Gnosticism.

Some go even further in defence of the teachings of mainstream Christianity and of opposition to Gnosticism. Robert Speer in his book *The Finality of Jesus Christ* writes somewhat tendentiously:

> That Christianity lives because it was true to the truth. Through all the centuries it has never been able to live otherwise. It cannot live otherwise today.

Chapter Seven:

Sophia, her Magic and the Serpent

Whichever religion – Judaeo-Christian or otherwise – we might subscribe to, there are certain images that have a particular resonance with what, thanks to C.G. Jung, is now known as the Collective Unconscious.

The Mythological Snake

The snake or serpent is such a potent image in creation myths that it is found in almost every religious and belief system. In Chapter Three we saw how Eurynome formed Ophion from the north wind. In Celtic myth the world originated from an egg which came from the mouth of a serpent, while in Babylonian myth the god Marduk overcame the dragon-like monster Tiamat so that he could form heaven and earth from the creature's body.

In the mythology of most of the world's peoples, a serpent or dragon is linked to the origin of the world and to creation – it is the primordial being, the still undivided unity that held sway before the creation of the world. In the Old Testament, victory over Rahab and the dragon meant that the mighty waters of the primeval deep were dried up.

Even today, the Native Americans of the northwest coast carry out certain winter rituals, when most of the sunlight has disappeared, that are directly linked to a primordial period. In a myth similar to a Gnostic one in which the light of Sophia is trapped in matter, the Native Americans believe that the sun has been imprisoned by the powers of darkness and water, which are symbolized by the serpent Sisul. In Indian mythology, Vasuki the world serpent is pulled this way and that by the gods and demons (*asuras*) so that Mandara, the world mountain that stands in the ocean of milk, is set in motion rather like a creative whisk. In Bronze Age myths, the serpent was thought to be the consort of the goddess who unites with her to bring fertility to the earth.

The serpent is said to know all mysteries. For instance, the children of Hecuba, queen of Troy, were licked by a serpent and received the gift of prophecy. This is possibly a reference to the technique which, in Eastern religions, is known as raising Kundalini. Kundalini means 'serpent fire' and the techniques:

> are designed to arouse the dormant power of the sleeping serpent (in all of us) by, firstly, awakening it from torpor and then getting it to raise its body upwards through each of the chakras (centres of psychic energy) until its head is in the ultimate sahasrara (crown of the head).

The sleeping serpent is the spiritual and psychic energy inherent in all of us and it is available when we make a commitment to the development which brings us into contact with the Divine. It shares similarities, therefore, with the divine spark we saw when the creation myths were discussed in Chapter Three.

Why then, in general terms, does the serpent appear in so many religions? One explanation is that it 'traces the spiralling of the life energy as it travels from one dimension to another'. It is easy, therefore, to see why snakes were associated with Athena, the Greek goddess of wisdom, in her role as strategist – and later, in the Middle Ages, with Prudentia, the personification of prudence or practical wisdom.

The scaly reptile can be a symbol of both death (as in the fall of man) and life (the brazen serpent). Its supposedly sinister character, with its attendant menace, brings about fear and its mysterious and duplicitous nature has led human beings to opposing assessments. On the one hand, it is thought of as evil and the cause of death and on the other it is believed to embody beneficial, and even divine, powers. It was as the wise one, in this beneficent form, that various sects of gnostics in late antiquity adored the godhead in the form of a serpent. These sects are generally grouped together under the name of Ophites.

Persian tradition tells of a plant called *baoma* that is said to have bestowed immortality; but Ahriman, Ahura Mazda's adversary, created a serpent that would harm the miraculous plant, thus casting the serpent on the side of evil. In the conflict between the two principles of being (good and evil) the realm of the divinity is often depicted by an eagle. The enmity between this divine bird and the snake is a theme in the mythology and art of many peoples. For instance, in later Christian artwork the eagle is a symbol of Christ and the serpent, dragon and basilisk are demonic animals. Before that, in Mithraic art, the figure that is usually interpreted as representing Aion, the god of time, was depicted with the head of a wolf and a body entwined by serpents.

Above all, however, the serpent has a lunar significance and therefore has a direct link with the feminine principle of God – Mircea Eliade speaks of it as 'an epiphany of the moon'. Like the moon that is gradually diminished and then slowly renews itself, so the serpent sheds and renews its skin and becomes a symbol of death and resurrection and the cycle of life.

The Gnostic Snake

In some Gnostic writings of the Hellenistic period there exists the notion that the first human beings crawled on the ground like snakes. Saturninos set out the Anthropos model of gnosis which maintains that no woman at all was present at the beginning. According to his system, the physical world was created by the seven angels or planets. At that time, the Unknown God revealed his own shining image, which was the Glory of heavenly man. Because the image withdrew from the physical world and returned to heaven at once, the angels were unable to hold onto it and so they attempted to fashion earthly man in a similar image.

However, this creature could not stand erect but slithered on the ground like a snake. The heavenly being (Adam) therefore sent his counterpart the spark of life, or the Spirit: this is now what leaves the physical body at death, allowing it to dissolve back into the earth. Mani relates a similar story, although there was ultimately a female entity, when he says that Primal Man – the Archanthropus – is sent to fight the powers of darkness. He is overcome and must leave 'the Maiden who is his soul' (perhaps Sophia) trapped by matter.

This cosmology would have been easily understood, even if perhaps not accepted, by people of the time, even if they adhered to different beliefs. For some, the earth was perceived as being surrounded by air and seven concentric spheres which were inhabited by the moon and six planets – only six because Uranus, although known, was not then recognized as a planet. (In his cosmology, Plato compared the spheres to a set of hemispherical bowls used by jugglers.) Beyond Saturn was the home of Leviathan, a coiled snake devouring its own tail for evermore. A similar image is presented by the *uroboros* (Greek for 'head in mouth'), the Gnostic serpent that swallows its own tail and is able to embrace the entire universe.

This serpent is somewhat different from the Leviathan that is described in the Old Testament:

> Can you draw out Leviathan with a fishhook, or press down his tongue with a cord? . . . Will he make many supplications to you? . . . Will he make a covenant with you to take him for your servant for ever? . . . Lay hands on him; think of the battle; you will not do it again! . . . No one is so fierce that he dares to stir him up . . . Who can open the doors of his face? His teeth are terrible round about. His back is made of rows of shields . . . His heart is hard as stone . . . Though the sword reaches him, it does not avail . . . He counts iron as straw, and bronze as rotten wood . . . His underparts are like sharp potsherds; he spreads himself like a threshing sledge on the mire. He makes the deep boil like a pot . . . Upon earth there is not his like, a creature without fear. (Job 41: 1–33)

This makes Leviathan sound more like a crocodile, or some other monster of the deep, that is summoned up like another of Jehovah's menaces. The prophet Isaiah describes the great powers threatening the people of God as a Leviathan – perhaps Babylon – and a dragon – perhaps Egypt.

According to Isaiah 27:1 (depending on how one wishes to interpret that particular passage) the Lord will slay Leviathan on the Day of Judgement:

> In that day the Lord will punish,
> With His great, cruel, mighty sword
> Leviathan the Elusive Serpent
> Leviathan the Twisting Serpent;
> He will slay the Dragon of the sea

This Leviathan is different again from the Leviathan in Hobbes's mid-seventeenth century work of political philosophy of that name, where it is used metaphorically. In *Leviathan*, Hobbes writes:

> . . . by art is created is created that great LEVIATHAN called a COMMONWEALTH, or STATE (in Latin, CIVITAS), which is but an artificial man, though of greater stature and strength than the natural, for whose protection and defence it was intended; and in which the sovereignty is an artificial soul, as giving life and motion to the whole body . . .

In our own day, the spiralling double helix form of DNA is another illustration of the serpent as Gnosis: this serpent is also blessed with a potential for healing. Two entwined snakes are an ancient symbol of Kundalini – the intermingling of the spiritual realms and the physical – and also the caduceus, a timeless symbol of healing. The umbilical cord is also significant in the way it resembles intertwined double snakes.

Again, the way in which the snake's movements contrast with its ability to appear completely lifeless during hibernation has been seen as a symbol for life and death by those close to nature, thus reinforcing the idea of the spiral of life energy.

In their book *The Myth of the Goddess*, Anne Baring and Jules Cashford observe:

> In the Neolithic age, as later in Minoan Crete, snakes and spirals (the snake in abstract form) are wound round vases and sculptures, coil over pregnant bellies, buttocks and phalluses, or undulate between moon, sun, stars and rain, as the dynamic principle of the life-energy that never runs out . . .

A figure that is not seen in early Christian art – although it can be observed at a later date – is that of the labyrinth. As a symbol, it is at least as important as snakes and serpents. It has become a representation of the inner journey to the centre of oneself which was initially the path of ignorance, but which later on became a tool for self-awareness – a prerequisite of Gnostic knowledge. As an enclosed structure it usually represented the mystery of the feminine ideal and the hidden aspects of femininity. It points us in the direction of the feminine aspect of God, which we saw in Chapter Three.

The path or structure of the labyrinth was often traced as a dance, suggesting the journey undertaken by the soul as it seeks to reunite with its own origin: thus creating a sacred space. The labyrinth was also often used as a magical device to protect and guard against the entry of hostile powers.

The Gnostic Worlds

In its best-known form, with seven concentric circles, the labyrinth may well have been a representation of the universe as it was then understood. Going back to the Gnostic structure of the universe, beyond Leviathan, it was thought that within those concentric planetary spheres were seven or twelve demons called Archons – the number depends on the source of your information. Beyond these was Paradise, which contained the Tree of Life and the flaming, turning sword mentioned in Genesis 3:24. The fixed stars, divided into the twelve signs of the zodiac, are in an outer space, the whole forming a kingdom called the Earthly Cosmos, the creation of the Demiurge, which in turn was Sophia's attempt at emanation.

> And when she saw (the consequences of) her desire, it changed into a form of a lion-faced serpent. And its eyes were like lightning fires which flash. She cast it away from her, outside that place, that no one of the immortal ones might see it, for she had created it in ignorance. And she surrounded it with a luminous cloud, and she placed a throne in the middle of the cloud that no one might see it except the holy Spirit who is called the mother of the living.

Inevitably, being Sophia's faulty emanation and therefore belonging to neither kingdom, the Demiurge, as the embodiment of evil, was only capable of manifesting a physical world that was also evil.

There are two other kingdoms. Sophia, because of her special duty to redeem the Earthly Cosmos, resides in a kingdom which is at an intermediate stage between her emanation and those of her Father. This is made up of inner blue darkness and outer yellow light. (In pictorial representations, Sophia is often shown wearing a blue gown edged with yellow which signifies her status as the queen of heaven; a status also occupied by Mary, the mother of Jesus.) The principal kingdom is the kingdom of God, which consists of two spheres. The outer sphere, that of the unknowable Supreme Being, was referred to in the *Apocryphon of St John* in this way:

> And I asked to know it, and he said to me, 'The Monad is a monarchy with nothing above it. It is he who exists as God and Father of everything, the invisible One who is above everything, who exists as incorruption, which is in the pure light into which no eye can look.'

The other one is the inner sphere of the Son. The Son must later unite with Sophia in order to fully redeem the world.

Gnostics did admit to the possibility of salvation. Some people's bodies were endowed with Sophia's divine spark and they were ready for salvation whatever their behaviour before death (pneumatics). Others might be saved if they embraced the doctrines of Gnosticism (psychics). Finally, there were the carnal ones (hylics) who were beyond redemption.

Creationists who accept the Judaeo-Christian view of how the universe began might ask, 'surely sin came into the world when Eve, tempted by the serpent, ate the apple from the tree of knowledge, despite having been told it was forbidden?' Not so, according to

Gnostics. They argue that the snake is a symbol of good, more liberator than seducer, bringing knowledge and everything else we understand as human into the world. The *Testimony of Truth* says:

> But the serpent was wiser than all the animals that were in Paradise, and he persuaded Eve, saying, 'On the day when you eat from the tree which is in the midst of Paradise, the eyes of your mind will be opened.'

To understand their reasoning, we should need to understand that those who wrote the Nag Hammadi scriptures were probably aware that Genesis was not a historical document but was, in fact, a myth. Today, in more prosaic terms, we would call Adam and Eve the personalizations of two principles. Adam was the personalization of the soul – the emotional, thinking functions of the personality, while Eve was the spirit or *pneuma* (spiritual consciousness or intuition).

There was a belief put forward in *On the Origin of the World* that the mystical Zoe (meaning 'life'), who manifests in the physical world as Eve, is the daughter and messenger of Sophia. In this case, Adam has no spiritual soul, but he is needed so that those whom he could father might also become carriers of the divine spark. It is Eve who commands Adam to live and to walk upright upon the Earth.

It is here that Gnostics decided that the creator god (Demiurge) could not have been a good god. Firstly, it would appear that he is jealous of Adam who, in eating the fruit of the Tree of Knowledge, put himself on a par with the Demiurge and acquired knowledge (*gnosis*). Secondly, the creator god is a jealous god who metes out punishment in short order. Thirdly, he cannot be quite so all-knowing since, when Adam and Eve hide, he cannot find them. The Gnostics of the time therefore came to the conclusion that there must be something beyond this evil being.

They not only decided that the Jewish god Jehovah was the

Demiurge (half maker), and was therefore imperfect, but they also believed that creation was basically a mistake. The Aeons and Sophia have been put in a position of having to contribute their light and power to this mistake until such time as it becomes perfect and can return to the Pleroma.

One other myth, which seems to have an element of truth about it, is told in the *Hypostasis of the Archons.* This suggests that the Flood was sent by the envious and spiteful creator in order to eradicate the larger part of its world, because people were become wiser and more discerning. Noah's wife, called Norea, is the daughter of Eve and therefore she is a 'knower of hidden things'. She does her best to prevent Noah from collaborating with the creator god.

Throughout this book, *gnosis* has been defined as knowledge and inner knowledge: it is defined here as a knower of hidden things. We have also defined it as intuitive knowledge. An example of intuitive knowledge is the situation in which one is asked the question 'How do you know?' only to answer 'I just do'.

The kind of transcendence that goes beyond empirical observation has, of course, always been the province of the feminine. It is this factor that has frightened people from time immemorial: it eventually led to the supposition that woman was evil. The Gnostics, by acknowledging that such a faculty is a necessary, if not magical, part of a successful existence upon this earth have restored the feminine to its rightful place.

All religions, including Gnosticism, have problems with the actual balance of power between the masculine and feminine elements and there are numerous worldwide myths about this conflict. Patriarchal religions would have it that the masculine is supreme whereas feminist thought has enabled women make an extremely good case for their own supremacy. In fact, the conflict could be very easily resolved if principles of equality were brought into play.

Whether we think of the masculine element as being the doer and the feminine element as being the instigator, or whether we think of the former as active and the latter as passive, really does not matter. It is when we achieve a balance between the two energies that we find it easier to think of a 'perfect world'. It is the balance of the physical and the spiritual that is important.

This does away with the distinction between the infinite creator and his finite creatures. Rather than a situation existing in which humans and animals are on earth while God is in heaven, with the two entities never meeting, there is a blend of energies which allows for co-operation and collaboration.

Magic and Mystery

It is this blending of energy that is epitomized by the six-pointed star now known as the Star of David. It is a protective device which seems to have become a Jewish symbol only as late as the seventeenth century, yet it was being used as an esoteric symbol long before then, in places such as Tibet and Egypt.

The upward pointing triangle is the physical realm (fire) reaching up towards the spiritual and the downwards pointing triangle is the spiritual realm of the waters of life reaching towards the Earth in order to lift it upwards. The symbol was first popularized by Kabbalists (Jewish mystics) and more recently it has been given a symbolic meaning for Gnostics by the Gnostic Association of the City of New York:

> The upright (red) triangle has been associated with the element Fire, not just fire as we perceive it physically, but the inner nature of fire from within the internal dimensions, which is responsible for the manifestation of physical fire in the first place. Without this prior manifestation of this inner nature of fire from within the internal dimensions of nature, fire, as we perceive it physically, could not even take place

> or manifest in the physical realm . . . The downward (blue) triangle has been associated with the element Water, Spiritual Water, that is, the Waters of Life. Both triangles now together, Spiritual Fire and Spiritual Water, make up what we call Conscience and Complete Enlightenment. There is a well-known formula in authentic esoteric schools: <Water> + <Fire> = <Enlightened Conscience>.

The star, incidentally, is an important image within many belief systems. The upward five-pointed star – the Pentagram – is an integral part of Pagan and Wiccan spell work. (This represents the Devil and its malign energy when reversed.) The eight-pointed star suggests knowledge or gnosis while the twelve-pointed star, while intrinsically unstable, is thought to symbolize the universe.

Kabbalah

By far the most potent contribution that has been made to Jewish thought by Gnosticism is provided by developments in the Kabbalah, a philosophical system which is said to predate any religion. In fact, it only became well known in the twelfth century AD, through the good offices of Isaac the Blind (c.AD 1160–1236). In essence, it is thought to be a set of precepts that were provided by the good Creator God so that people could improve their lives and achieve fulfilment. Charles Poncé, in his book *Kabbalah. An Introduction and Illumination for the World Today*, writes that the term translates literally into tradition, specifically the tradition of Jewish mysticism. This he defines as:

> . . . an extension and amplification of traditional religious views. It attempts to go beyond or behind traditional dogma, in order to satisfy the needs which certain individuals have to experience the Divine directly, without the intercession of an appointed body of 'fathers'.

The suppression of Kabbalah as heresy was probably due to its magical elements rather than its spiritual dimension. Orthodox Jews were fearful of it leading to anti-Semitism and persecution and the idea of God having a female companion was anathema to them.

A wide variety of terms were used for those who studied the tradition of Kabbalah: children of faith; children of the king's palace; masters of knowledge; masters of mystery; men of belief; those who know; those who know grace; those who know wisdom; those who reap the field; and those who have entered and left, to name but a few. These all have a peculiarly Gnostic ring to them.

A traditional Kabbalistic view is that although the creation is in a damaged and imperfect state the Kabbalist, by virtue of his or her state of consciousness, can bring about a real healing. The principal root of Kabbalistic tradition is the *Torah* (the law), which was created prior to the formation of mankind. When Moses first received the written law he also received certain laws orally. These were not written down but only ever transmitted down through the generations by word of mouth, and then only to the initiated. This oral law is sometimes referred to as Kabbalah. Incidentally, there are several different spellings of this word, because some letters in Hebrew have more than one representation in English and they have different magical vibrations with greater or lesser impact.

Much of the magical language that we use today has come down to us from the Kabbalah. It was recognized that there were certain ideas that the ordinary layman was capable of understanding and others which only the initiated were capable of assimilating. Knowledge was power and that knowledge must be jealously guarded lest it fall into the wrong hands. If anything was written down it was recorded in such a way that only those with the required knowledge would be able to decipher the true meaning. The writings were therefore in code. These coded messages had a tremendous power and energy invested in them and the sense of awe and wonder that they generated was phenomenal. In fact, the messages are still able to generate that same sense of awe and wonder when they become open to interpretation in modern times.

Two strands run through Kabbalistic thought: one is esoteric while the other is more practical. Together they offer a coherent method of handling the world in which its adherents live. The *Torah* is believed to be divine, to have hidden meanings and to have divine power concealed within it. The *Zohar* is a series of documents covering a huge variety of subjects, from esoteric interpretation to discussions on the nature of God; it was highly significant in mainstream Jewish thought and indeed it still is today. By studying the relevant texts and following certain precepts, one is able to unlock the secrets of creation. Some Kabbalists therefore believe that they have inherited practical techniques from the biblical prophets – there is also a belief by some that Pythagoras received his erudition from Hebrew sources.

Kabbalah neither attempts to define God nor does it tell the individual what he or she should believe. It does assume, however, that some level of direct experience of God is feasible and it gives practical methods for achieving this. Ritual has always been an integral part of Kabbalah, which has successfully integrated techniques from cultures and traditions all over the world. One of its prime teachings is that similar techniques can be used to achieve both thaumaturgy and theurgy – it is only the intention which is different.

Contact with the divine (theurgy) often brings about the perception of spiritual beings and angels. Angels are found in the Judaic, Christian, Islamic and Zoroastrian traditions. In common with the groupings of the Aeons, they are often thought of as being in congregations of four, seven or twelve. This demonstrates their connection with the channelling of energy from the divine via the planets – an old concept that goes back as far as Plato. Two of the archangels deserve particular mention in the Gnostic context:

- Michael is said to be at war with the serpent or great dragon. This is often identified with Samael (the blind god), who was an aspect of Ialdeboth the Demiurge. Uriel is the bringer of Truth. His association with light is significant because of the importance of light in practical Kabbalah, which echoes the cultivation of the divine spark. A number of different kinds of light are identified, including: nogah (glow), tov (good), bahir (brilliant), zohar (radiant), kavod (glory), chaim (life), and muvhak (scintillating).
- Samael also has importance, though for a different reason. He appears in various guises as the Dark Angel and the Angel of Death. He is consistently associated with the planet Mars and is thought to be the source of all the evil in the world. Identified with the serpent in the Garden of Eden, he is a tempter and a poisoner of life and the suffix -el demonstrates his divine origin. Some Kabbalists put him at the head of a demonic hierarchy while others view him as a source of malign energy that requires containment.

One myth of creation which belongs to the Kabbalah is as follows:

God 'compressed' himself in a process of self-limitation in order to accommodate his new creation. This contraction took place in the *En Soph* – the limitless, unknown and unknowable God. The Light, entering this space in a stream, emanated the *sephiroth* (vessels of power). All except the first three were shattered by the power of the light: this breaking of the vessels is called '*shevirah*'. The shards of the broken vessels fell into the abyss created by the contraction and formed the '*qelippot*' – a sort of negative mirror of the sephiroth. Most of the light returned to the *En Soph* (the Ultimate), but some of it remained caught in the vessels and fell with the *qelippot*. This particular aspect of the story shares similarities with the return of the spiritual Adam to the light as mentioned in Chapter Six.

One way of looking at the *shevirah* is that it might have been a corrective action in which the unbalanced powers of Judgement, the broken vessels, were ejected into the abyss because evil was present in such quantities that balance could only be restored in this way.

Whether it was a catharsis or a blunder, the *shevirah* was cataclysmic: nothing was as it should have been. The four interlinking worlds of Kabbalah slipped when they should have been held stable and the lowest world descended into the world of the shells. Much of the Kabbalah taught by Isaac Luria (1534–1572) is concerned with the corrective actions needed for the sparks of light trapped in the realm of the shells to be freed so that creation can be perfected.

Hermeticism

Another system that should perhaps be fitted into the Gnostic framework is Hermeticism. It is very diverse and it draws its material from many sources within the Western Mystery traditions; it considers that the whole of mankind is on a spiritual journey that is designed to return to a state of unity with the Mind of God and this state of unity is its prime purpose; and it holds that spiritual growth cannot be achieved without human effort. If humanity is to reach the Divine, therefore, we must aspire to the Divine.

Hermeticism takes its name from the God Hermês Trismegistos (Greek for 'Thrice-Greatest Hermes'), who was reputed to be a Græco-Egyptian sage of Thôth, the Egyptian God of Wisdom and Magic. However, in the early fifteenth century it was posited that far from being the work of one man, Hermeticism was a collection of the writings of scholars from Alexandria in the second and third centuries AD – that is, the writings were created at roughly the same time as the Nag Hammadi texts.

As both a form of philosophy and a set of rules by which to live, Hermeticism has survived many changes and there has been a great resurgence of interest in the present day. Its main tenets are that:

- The Divine creation of the Universe is ultimately good.
- Spiritual and magical practices such as theurgy, meditation and ritual should be used as a regular practice in order to attain access to the higher realms of knowledge.
- The Divine is both within and yet beyond everything.
- In coming to terms with all things a natural balance can be sought.
- It upholds the search for spiritual meaning.
- The Divine can be found in the Mysteries of Nature.
- There is a natural rhythm to life. There is no necessity for self-denial.
- It is polytheistic – arises from many Expressions of the Divine – yet it is also ultimately monotheistic (it comes from one source).

Both Hermeticism and Kabbalah would appear to be systems of magic to the uninitiated. Each system works on the assumption that spiritual awareness is more important than power over the mundane; so they show the influence of their non-Christian beginnings.

A kind of amalgamation of the two systems has come into being over the last 500 years. Whether or not this conforms to the spirit of the original Jewish Kabbalah it is difficult to say. Once again, it is the intent behind the study and practice which decides whether these systems fit into Gnostic thought for each individual.

Alchemy

In many ways it was the Kabbalah, a necessary part of knowledge, which was the vehicle for one of the most important aspects of medieval thought, that of alchemy. Here we have the paradox of Gnosticism being regenerated by Jews, Christians and Muslims after having been dubbed a heresy by orthodox monotheists,.

If you have always thought that alchemy was a kind of 2,500-year-old magic that is concerned with the conversion of copper and lead into silver and gold with the help of the philosopher's stone, you would only be partially right. In fact, alchemists found it convenient to have people think this, because what they were actually searching for was the secret of life, or rather how creation began. The stories which grew up about the creation of *homunculi* (little men) were evidence of the alchemists' faulty attempts at creation – what we would call genetic engineering in the present day.

Alchemists were obviously feared and reviled, so any attempt to profit from what they had learned would be the object of suspicion. Admittedly, the idea of making a fortune by transmuting base metals lasted until the nineteenth century. Even then, alchemist Mary Anne Atwood was able to define alchemy, with lip-service paid to science as:

> a universal art of vital chemistry which by fermenting the human spirit purifies and finally dissolves it. . . . Alchemy is philosophy; it is the philosophy, the finding of the Sophia in the mind.

Scientists from Newton onwards had begun to distance themselves from both the inadequate chemistry and the mysterious cosmology of alchemy. However, some philosophers were attracted to the mystical side of alchemy as an alternative to the 'mechanistic' science of the day.

It was alchemists who first developed the use of symbols to designate certain substances in their experiments – substances that might be harmful if they fell into the wrong hands. For instance, it was thought that mercury sulphate – a combination of the esoteric aspects of Mercury (symbolizing Spiritual Water) and Sulphur (symbolizing Fire) – was a part of the information needed to assist the soul's migration back to its source. This, of course, brings us directly back to the Seal of Solomon, which is now more commonly known as the Star of David.

You can find the influence of alchemy in the legends of the Holy Grail and Dante's poetry – it can even be seen in the Porch of Judgement at the entrance to Notre Dame cathedral in Paris, where the figure of Alchemy sits below that of Christ. It can also be seen in the love songs of troubadours – lyric poets who, between the eleventh and thirteenth centuries, took the message of Sophia and union with the Divine all over Europe in the Provençal tongue of Languedoc. It is also seen in the concept of the Black Virgin, black being the colour most often associated with Wisdom. To medieval heresy-hunters the troubadours appeared to be propagandists for heresy disguised as entertainers; they were killed according to the instruction of the Christian church at more or less the same time as the Cathars were put down in France.

Gnostic Astrology

For the alchemists, the timing of their experiments was often of crucial importance as was the correct placing of influences on those experiments. This required an extensive knowledge of the ancient art of astrology in order that they could minimize external factors when conducting their experiments.

Because the belief at the time was that the planets had been created by the Aeons (emanations of God) and were dedicated to assisting the earth plane to escape from entrapment, it was very easy to perceive that using the good offices of the planets was the right thing to do. In other words, the alchemists were calling on the powers of the universe to assist them in the search for the meaning of life. As mathematics and science became more and more complex, their calculations would need to be precise and exact. Those early alchemists were able to carry out complex calculations such as multiple measurements, arithmetic and algebra – operations that today are given over to computers.

According to Gnostic thought, each Aeon and planet had been given a particular realm of responsibility by the Father (good) God for life within this Earth. It was, therefore, easy to personalize those qualities by creating intermediary gods, just as the early Greeks did. For the uninitiated, the gods themselves became more important than the planetary influences, although the initiated would have understood that they must in the end be spiritually transformed.

In the early twentieth century, Carl Jung came to the conclusion that alchemy was a symbolic system for spiritual transformation as well as a psychological tool. At around the same time, the theosophist Gurdjieff recognized that the human body had the potential to be the alchemical receptacle that transmutes lower into higher energies. Astrology, therefore, was a vital tool in understanding this 'human' alchemy.

It is almost certain that all cultures have their own version of astrology and that they all subscribe to the idea that different influences affect the earth plane and its inhabitants. Also, they each have their own version of the creation myth. Central to most of these versions is the idea that the dual aspects of light and dark have a meaning which has, as yet, not been totally understood on an esoteric level.

Not to be confused with the watered-down version that is promoted by the popular media, astrology was – and still remains – an important part of the way of being of many peoples. For instance, groups as divergent as Pagans, Mandeans, Hermeticists and Kabbalists – even some scientists – recognize that the measurement of the stars does have a validity today.

Chapter Eight:

Persecution and Propaganda

When following the course of Gnosticism, one of the problems that has to be overcome is that of gaining a true account of what really took place. The early writers of church history were patently so concerned that their own doctrines might be suspect that the rigorous anti-heresy bias, rather than being a statement of fact, comes across as an act of suppression.

According to Origen, whom we have already mentioned, only a small number of Christians were in evidence in the first two centuries. Dion Cassius, who wrote the history of Rome in eighty volumes during the latter part of the second century, does not mention either Christians or Christian Churches, although it was at around this time that Christianity was beginning to be recognized. By the fourth century, however, there are still only about six lines relating to the Christians in a compilation of the Augustan Library (part of which had been accomplished earlier, during the reign of Constantine). Plutarch, initiated into the mysteries of the Greek god Apollo, and for a time one of the two priests of Apollo at the Oracle of Delphi, is silent on Christianity.

Criticism and Courage

In the early days of Christianity, Iranaeus (AD 130–202) appears to be the most vociferous opponent of Gnosticism. He wrote *On the Detection and Overthrow of the So-Called Gnosis*, which is normally referred to as *Adversus Haereses* (English: *Against Heresies*). This book does its best to refute the teachings of various Gnostic groups and until the discovery of the Nag Hammadi texts it was considered to be the best surviving description of Gnostic faith.

Iraenaeus demonstrates for us the diversity of Christian belief at the time, since his own theology postulates that Jesus would have had to live through to old age in order to be the saviour of mankind. Oddly, he puts forward the theory that Adam and Eve were created children, so their fall from Grace was nothing but a childish spat that reflected the desire to have everything immediately, while expressing the need to grow up.

Tertullian lived at about the same time as Iraeneus and it is quite difficult to assess his view of Gnosticism. His writings cover the whole theological field of the time: apologetics against paganism and Judaism; polemics; polity; discipline; and morals, or the whole reorganization of human life on a Christian basis. It seems that he had initially converted to Christianity and then become a Montanist – a cult that began in the second century and that allegedly preached from direct revelation of the Holy Spirit. It is difficult, therefore, to accommodate his bile against Marcion with his defence of religious freedom since he said:

> There is a natural law and a man-made law that each person should be free to worship whom he wants. One man's religion does not harm another's. It is not for religion to compel religion. Gods do not desire unwilling sacrifice.

Tatian is another early historian who is worth studying. He was vehemently opposed to paganism, but he seems to have had an intimate knowledge of Valentinus' teachings. He taught that creation began from the *dynamis logike* ('power expressed in words'). From God came the Logos who was generated in the beginning in order to produce the world by creating the matter from which the whole of creation was formed. This was then penetrated by the *pneuma hylikon* ('world spirit') which is common to angels, stars, Man, animals and plants. This world spirit is less than the divine *pneuma* and in man is the *psyche* or 'soul'. Essentially, therefore, Man does not differ from animals except that he has a special relationship with the divine spirit, which raises him above the animals. It is this spirit that is the image of God, and it is this that gives him his immortality.

Tatian was the first to give the Syriac congregations the Gospel in their own language. Although he perhaps did not give them their ascetic practices, he certainly enhanced them. He taught that baptism consisted of taking a vow of celibacy which, once made, was sacrosanct for life.

Monasticism

Celibacy was obviously not something to which everyone could aspire, but for those who were capable of complete celibacy there was another way. Christianity gradually became more organized and the different beliefs were standardized into a form that was acceptable to the masses. In the Roman Catholic Church, celibacy became a requirement for those who wanted to become priests, in accordance with the words of Jesus. (Matthew 19: 12) By the fifth century AD, monasticism gave those who required it some kind of sanctuary and a direct line of access to God. As a result, there was less necessity for Gnostic thought with its sharp divisions between good and evil, the spiritual and the physical.

Bogomils

That is not to say that gnosticism disappeared altogether, contrary to popular belief; it simply went underground. The Bogomils were without a doubt the connecting link between the so-called heretical sects of the East and those of the West – they were also the most active in spreading their teachings to Russia and the rest of Europe. Choosing to deny the divine birth of Jesus and the personal coexistence of the Son with the Father and the Holy Ghost, they also had no truck with sacraments and ceremonies. They identified with the teachings of Paul and Mani and also became known as Paulicians. By the eleventh century the Bogomils were well established in Bulgaria. This later led to the development of the Paulicians.

Albigensians

The Albigensians were an offshoot of the Paulicians and opinions differ as to whether they were a branch of what became known as the Cathars or vice versa. The Albigenses were truly Gnostic in that they believed in the coexistence of two opposing principles – one good, the other evil. Good is the creator of the spiritual world and evil the material world. The bad principle is the source of all ordinary, natural phenomena. This evil principle created the human body and is the perpetrator of sin, which springs from matter and not from the spirit. Earthly life, therefore, was evil and marriage and the perpetuation of life were equally so.

Only the *perfecti* submitted to the full rigour of this stricture – the majority of their followers lived ordinary human lives. So indoctrinated were the followers that they saw the *perfecti* as being beyond reproach and they lived in the hope that they would be given the grace to renounce all gratification of the flesh and receive 'the *consolamentum*' before death.

> They call the laying-on of hands the consolamentum, spiritual baptism, or baptisms of the Holy Spirit. Without it according to them, mortal sin cannot be forgiven, and the Holy Spirit cannot be conferred on anyone: it is given only by them, through the consolamentum. On this the Albaneses differ somewhat from the others. They say that the hand contributes nothing (since according to them it was created by the devil, as we shall see), and it is only the Lord's Prayer said by whoever performs the ceremony that is effective.
> (Ranier Sacchoni, 1250)

The supreme act of heroism, as suggested by the leaders of the sect, was to starve oneself to death (known as *endura)* and so be free of matter altogether. Such a practice caused a great deal of distress to a number of people, but since no secret was made of the Albigensian doctrine the persecution they suffered did not come initially from the Church. It came more from the sense of outrage and anger that was felt by those who knew about it and had been affected by it.

Because the practices of the Albigensians were not only felt to be incompatible with the peace and welfare of mankind but were also the subject of propaganda, Pope Innocent III was led to mount a campaign against them in 1209. This became known as the Albigensian Crusade. At first the greatest leniency was used – only when the Albigenses (having little regard for human life) had apparently assassinated the Papal legate were stricter measures used.

The Cathars

The last surviving ruins of the Cathar Gnostic school in the south of France near Toulouse, in Languedoc, are now a tourist attraction. The so-called sacred mountain of Montségur, and the meadow beneath, the Field of the Burned, were the places where the remnants of the

Cathars (Greek for 'pure'), branded heretics by the Catholic Church, were brutally disposed of in March 1244. The story is as follows: Simon de Montfort used Pope Innocent III's Albigensian Crusade as an opportunity to acquire territory for himself in France. At the Siege of Beziers in 1209 the 'crusaders' had seized the town in less than an hour. Immediately there began a mass slaughter of both Catholics and Cathars. When asked how they could distinguish between Catholics and Cathars, de Montfort replied, 'Kill them all; God will know his own'.

By 1244 the hounding of the Cathars had been so successful that those Cathari who would not renounce their faith had taken refuge at Montségur. They were forced to surrender. Having asked for time to prepare – possibly to celebrate one of their major festivals on the previous day – 205 parfaits marched singing to their deaths on the sixteenth of March.

It seems that four of the initiates escaped that night – they took treasure with them including, it is said, the Holy Grail (the cup used by Jesus at the Last Supper). The Cathari papers were burned with the martyrs, so the only record of Cathari beliefs that survives today is in documents of the Inquisition. A testament to their martyrdom in the shape of a solar cross is still in existence on what was their site – with the words

'Be Thou Perfect'.

In theory it should have been possible for the Cathars to live peaceably with other people. Everyone, even local aristocrats, seemed to get on with them because they posed no obvious threat. However, their talent for democracy, which showed in a practice of tolerance and personal freedom, irritated a rich and worldly Catholic Church that was disappointed at the failure of the Crusades. It became concerned that Catharism might catch on and still further affect its dominant position. Persecution was inevitable, having been accorded validity by the Inquisition, and the die was cast.

Cathari beliefs were typically Gnostic. Bertrand Russell described them thus:

> It seems that the Cathari were dualists . . . they considered the Old Testament Jehovah a wicked demiurge, the true God being only revealed in the New Testament. They regarded matter as essentially evil, and believed that for the virtuous there is no resurrection of the body. The wicked, however, will suffer transmigration into the bodies of animals. On this ground they were vegetarians, abstaining even from eggs, cheese, and milk. They ate fish, however, because they believed that fishes are not sexually generated. All sex was abhorrent to them . . . they saw no objection in suicide. They accepted the New Testament more literally than did the orthodox; they abstained from oaths, and turned the other cheek. . . . The stricter precepts of the sect were only to be observed by certain exceptionally holy people called the 'perfected'; The others might eat meat and even marry.

The Cathari believed that because Jesus was cosmic he could not have been crucified. They also thought that woman was man's equal but could not preach. For the parfaits, marriage, baptism and communion were not recognized as they were not part of core Gnostic rituals.

Incidentally, the *Catholic Encyclopaedia* claims the opposite, bringing attention to the idea of induction or initiation:

> All Gnostic sects possessed this rite in some way; in Mandaeism daily baptism is one of the great practices of the

> system. The formulae used by Christian Gnostics seemed to have varied widely from that enjoyed by Christ. The Marcosians said: 'In the name of the unknown Father of all, in the Truth, the Mother of all, in him, who came down on Jesus'. The Elcesaites said: 'In the name of the great and highest God and in the name of his Son, the great King'. In Irenaeus we find the formula: 'In the name that was hidden from every divinity and lordship and truth, which (name) Jesus the Nazarene has put on in the regions of light' and several other formulae, which were sometimes pronounced in Hebrew or Aramaic. The Mandaeans said: 'The name of the Life and the name of the Manda d'Haye is named over thee'. In connection with Baptism the Sphragis was of great importance; in what the seal or sign consisted wherewith they were marked is not easy to say. There was also the tradition of a name either by utterance or by handing a tablet with some mystic word on it.

In common with the Albigensians, the Cathari carried out the ritual of *consolamentum*. In this they differ from other sects. The rite is described by Judith Mann:

> This ceremony consisted of the Parfait laying his hands upon the head of the literally dying or upon the head of the believer who aspired to enter the community of the Parfaits. A transmission of immense vivifying energy was said to take place, inspiring to those who witnessed it. The ritual of the Consolamentum may have strongly contributed to the rapid spread of Catharism. This energy transmission allowed the spirit to continue its ascent towards the Light in safety, to evolve, or if the recipient was on the threshold of death, to make the leap into the

> cosmos. To not fear death was a crowning achievement. This courage served the adepts well when they were ruthlessly hunted down.

This vivifying energy is a transmission of pure spiritual power and might be recognized today as being akin to a strong healing energy or an energy that is transmitted by some Gurus and holy men. The Cathars obviously knew how to use the energy of the natural world, for the perfects (parfaits) worshipped in the open air, in forests and on mountains. Their initiation ceremonies took place in the region's limestone caves near Pic de St Barthalemy. Judith Mann fills in the detail:

> The sacred caves of the Sabarthez cluster around the small resort town of Ussat-les-Bains and are known as 'doors to Catharism'. To reach Bethlehem, the most important of the Cave Churches of Ornolac, one must climb the steep Path of Initiation. The Cave of Bethlehem may well have been the spiritual centre of the Cathar world. For it was here that the 'pure' candidate underwent an initiation ceremony that culminated in the Consolamentum. Four aspects of the Cave were used in the ceremony:
>
> A square niche in the wall in which stood the veiled Holy Grail
> A granite altar upon which The Gospel of John lay
> A pentagram hewn into the wall
> Telluric currents emanating from the rock walls and floor.

The Mandaeans have already been mentioned as an ancient Gnostic sect that has survived persecution in Iraq without causing much fuss outside. So how and why did this other equally historical 'modern' sect, the Cathari, land up in France in the first place?

The Cathari traced their roots back to Marcion and to the Paulicians, After merging with the Bogomiles they went into Bulgaria and finally appeared in France. By the time they arrived near Toulouse, in a region which was even then called Oc, they had centres in Italy, Bosnia, Croatia, Switzerland and Germany as well as Bulgaria. At one time there were 40,000 believers (croyants) and 1000 priests (parfaits).

Croyants, who lived in houses run by an elder or prioress, could become parfaits after three years apprenticeship. Parfaits tended to lead ordinary lives and help with the chores, living on what they earned. They had no special rights, did not believe in any feudal hierarchy, preached in the local language – the *langue d'Oc* ('language of yes'; *oc* was local word for yes) – and promoted feminism and equality for the poor.

Politicking within the established church, and the rise of fanaticism, meant that anything that did not fit in with orthodox thought had to be eradicated. The church believed that the heresy had to be stopped, and it was: bloodily. The Cathar influence however lived on.

Dr Francis King, citing Dr Arthur Guirdham's own earlier books, in his *Encyclopaedia of Mind, Magic and Mythical Stories*, says that Guirdham:

> claims that the souls of Cathar heretics walk the earth today, reincarnated in the bodies of the men and women around us. Furthermore, destiny has ensured that the bodies of those heretics burned at the stake or put to the sword in 13th century France have been able to meet up with each other some 700 years after the last encounter.

Interestingly, because he feels that he has sufficient subjective evidence, Dr Guirdham, risking ridicule even in today's more tolerant society, goes so far as to believe that:

> the bodies of several of his friends and patients housed the reincarnated souls of medieval heretics.

Whether or not we believe him, his book has certainly strengthened the beliefs of those occultists who regard the Cathars as custodians of a secret-wisdom religion and would class them as martyrs. One might wonder, however, whether it is the knowledge of the Divine which makes itself felt in the present day or the personalities of the parfaits.

Knights Templar

Just prior to the time when the Cathars were being butchered, the Knights Templar were beginning to move into Europe. In 1118, during the reign of Baldwin II, Hugues de Payens, a knight of Champagne, and eight companions bound themselves by a perpetual vow to defend the Christian travellers. This was taken in the presence of the Patriarch of Jerusalem. More monastic than anything else, the Knights Templar closely aligned themselves with the Cistercians. They developed the order much like an army, with four ranks:

1. The *knights* who were equipped like the heavy cavalry of the Middle Ages and who operated according to the laws of Chivalry.
2. The *sergeants*, who formed the light cavalry.
3. The *farmers*, entrusted with the administration of temporals.
4. The *chaplains*, who alone were vested with holy orders, to minister to the spiritual needs of the order.

These last two were non-fighting ranks.

In due course the Templars achieved a great deal of wealth and fame. Almost inevitably they were accused of using corrupt practices and fell into disrepute. Dr. King states:

> Others have acquired unorthodox religious beliefs through

> their trading contacts with the east. A good many of the Knights must have at some time encountered the adherents of dualistic cults like Catharism . . . One such cult is said to have involved the worship of a deity named Baphomet. It has been said that Baphomet is merely a corrupt version of Mahomet – in other words that some Templars were converts to Islam. Others have argued that the name is a Latin derivation of a Greek phrase meaning 'baptism of wisdom' (Sophia?) and that the Templars were Gnostic initiates.

Baphomet is claimed by some to be a personalization of Satan. The originator of this story is said to have been their persecutor, Philip the Fair of France. Interestingly, the Templars were celibate, but their overriding vanity was pride in power.

The Templars certainly used initiation in their organization and it was this very fact that resulted in their downfall. These ceremonies were so secret that many myths grew up about their form. When such ceremonies were entrusted to the sergeants, however, they were often not carried out according to the prescribed order and corruption set in. Philip the Fair used the opportunity to mount a campaign against the Templars which, after the Pope had annulled one enquiry, ultimately resulted in the trial of the remaining members – not just in France, but across the whole of Europe.

Here, in a story that is similar to that of the Cathars, it is said that certain of the knights escaped from the terrible torture that was inflicted on them and hid much treasure somewhere in the vicinity of Rennes le Chateau. This is still being searched for to this day.

We come up against something of a problem when we examine the Knights Templar order. It is very easy to make the assumption that heresy is Gnosticism and vice versa. It is worthwhile remembering that an organization can be heretical or accused of heresy without being Gnostic.

There is a strong possibility that there was an association between the Templars and the Cathari, but it is not a foregone conclusion that the former were truly Gnostic – that is, that they sought knowledge of the Wisdom of the Divine and a contest between Good and Evil.

Alchemy and the Alchemists

One group of people who could not be ignored by the authorities were the alchemists, those searchers after the secrets of the Universe. Alchemy has been defined as 'any imaginary power or process of transmuting one thing into another'. Alchemy is also, as we explored briefly earlier, an integrated system of symbols and metaphors, sacred geometries, elements and heavenly bodies, personalizations and myths designed to provide help in understanding the nature of the Universe, while at the same time concealing information which could not be understood by the uninitiated.

Alchemy is based on an understanding of the universe that was first Hellenistic and later medieval. Nowadays, however, it is also accepted that it represents aspects of the human psyche and spirit as well – so that it is a truly Gnostic science. Linking to the four elements (earth, air, water and fire) and their four qualities (cold, hot, moist, and dry) the alchemist tries to achieve a transmutation of the elements in order to produce a fifth element, that of *Aether* or spirit. Pythagorus stated that the quaternity (the four) delineates the plethora of possibilities in the physical world. However there had to have been a fifth quality to hold everything together and it was Aristotle who posited the fifth element, the quintessence.

If this fifth element could be captured, then the secret of life could be revealed. Several processes are followed when dealing with substances in alchemy, but the end result is the Lapis or elixir that appears when the transformed elements are reunited and the work is completed. This is said to be the embodiment of the perfection of matter and spirit and the epitome of creation.

The table below shows the processes in an easily understood fashion.

The Alchemical Opus or Great Work

Order	Stage	Description
1	*Calcinatio*	Reduction of solid metal to powder or ash by roasting
2	*Solutio*	This ash is dissolved in water and purified by washing; '*solve et coagula*'
3	*Separatio*	It is then separated into its component parts and the spirit or watery vapour is released from the body or earthy matter
4	*Conjunctio*	Bringing together the substance of sulphur which represents the sun or masculine and Mercury (as the feminine or moon) there is a Mystic marriage which joins them together
5	*Putrefactio*	The product of this union must die and become blackened in order to transmute. This is called *nigredo*
6	*Ablutio*	There must then be a washing or baptism, which reveals the true colours and energies known as *cauda pavonis* or peacocks tail
7	*Albedo*	At this point the white elixir or stone is produced. This is what is known as the Philosopher's Stone
8	*Rubedo*	Finally the red elixir, the elixir of immortality and the culmination of the *opus* is achieved

It is very easy to see how such work could be misunderstood and how it would be seen as heretical, yet alchemists had in fact worked out the processes of creation. If energy is put under extreme pressure – heat, cold or density – it tends to become liquid, then solid and finally gaseous. Reverse that process and you have the art of manifestation. The idea was that by creating the elixir of life the alchemist would live for ever. If he transmuted lead into gold then that was a bonus.

Writing in the eighteenth century, General Hitchcock, an alchemist himself, said:

> The Alchemists (and all Philosophic Initiates of whatever school) were reformers in their time (Luther, Paracelsus, Agrippa, Andrea, Cagliostro, Saint Germaine, Boyle, Ramsey, Paine, Franklin, Clymer, LaFayette, and many others), obliged to work in secret and unknown at the time, nevertheless making history and their impression upon the public (for which the public was thankful in due time). For the most part they lived in ages when an open expression of their opinions, and knowledge of their efforts, would have brought them into conflict with the superstitions [and bigotry] of the times, and exposed them to all manner of persecution, even the rack and the stake; where, indeed, many of them did perish, not being sufficiently guarded in their language.

In the seventeenth century, Thomas Vaughan, another alchemist, patently demonstrates his allegiance to God and his wish to help others in their search. Although we might imagine the stereotypical alchemist as an old man with a beard, that does not apply here as Thomas Vaughan states that he is in his 'three and twentieth year'! He also holds out hope for the future:

> I being an adept anonymous, a lover of learning, and philosopher, decreed to write this little treatise of medicinal, chemical, and physical secrets in the year of the world's redemption 1645, in the three and twentieth year of my life, that I may pay my duty to the Sons of the Art, that I might appear to other adepts as their brother and equal. Therefore I presage that not a few will be enlightened by these my labours. These are no fables, but real experiments that I have made and know, as every other adept will conclude by these lines. In truth, many times I laid aside my pen, deciding to forbear from writing, being rather willing to have concealed the truth under a mask of envy. But God compelled me to write, and Him I could in no wise resist who alone knows the heart and unto whom be glory forever. I believe that many in this last age of the world will be rejoiced with the Great Secret, because I have written so faithfully, leaving of my own will nothing in doubt for a young beginner. I know many already who possess it in common with myself and are persuaded that I shall yet be acquainted in the immediate time to come. May God's most holy will be done therein. I acknowledge myself totally unworthy of bringing those things about, but in such matters I submit in adoration to Him, to whom all creation is subject, who created All to this end, and having created, preserves them.

In true Gnostic fashion, the alchemists were aware that the capacity for creation and the capacity for destruction were very finely balanced – nowhere more so than in themselves. Whoever held the secret of life had a power for evil that was as great as his power for good. These were the men who ultimately understood the symbolism of the prime rule of alchemy: use only one vessel, one fire and one instrument, which is the self. Through their work they were aware of the Power of their own Being. They knew the characteristics of the Secret Fire, the serpent power that moves upwards in spirals and of the great primitive force hidden in all matter both organic and inorganic.

Sacred Geometry

In looking to understand that primitive force, they would begin to understand the relevance of mathematics, of proportion and ratio. It is known that such figures as Pythagoras, Kepler (mathematician and astronomer) and Leonardo were all educated in Sacred Geometries and all held many beliefs about them and their role in the Universe.

Most alchemists would have needed a working knowledge of such beliefs. They would also have understood the idea of a solid representing a principle, since they would be well versed in the idea that numbers have a specific vibration. To experience a flavour of their knowledge, we can look at Platonic solids. These were first described by the Greeks and named in Plato's honour.

There are five, and only five, regular Platonic solids – that is solids bounded by plane figures such as triangles and squares – each with a particular esoteric or magical significance. All sides are equal, all angles are the same and all faces are identical. In each corner of such a solid the same number of surfaces collide. These are the Tetrahedron, Cube, Octahedron, Dodecahedron and Icosahedron, respectively.

 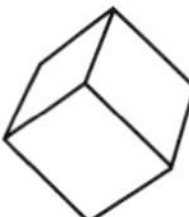   

The Tetrahedron represents the concept of system. When four radiating points interact, they will form the Tetrahedron. It has four triangular faces, and it is the structural basis for geodesic (earth-based) architecture. It has been associated with the element Fire.

The Cube or Hexahedron represents the three-dimensional, physical, manifest world, with its four directions (expressed by squares), right angles and polarities. It has six faces and has been associated with the element Earth.

The Octahedron has a dual relationship to the Cube. Whereas the Cube has six faces and eight vertices, the Octahedron has eight faces and six vertices. It has been associated with the element Air.

The Icosahedron has twenty triangular faces and twelve vertices. It is also considered to be a primary geodesic structure. It has been associated with the element Water.

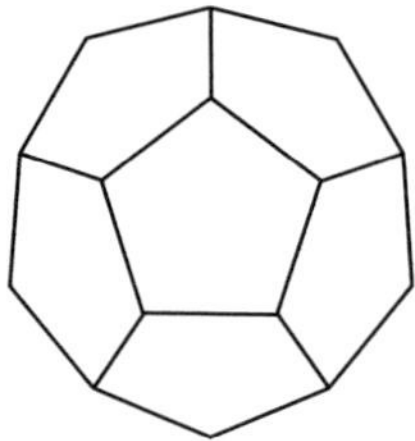

The Dodecahedron is the solid of most interest to alchemists. Historically it has symbolized the concept of a fifth element: Ether (*Aether*) or Universe. It represents the perfect intermingling of the infinite and the finite, the sphere and the cube – in flat form, the circle and the square. Some have believed that the Dodecahedron represents an idealized form of Divine thought, will or idea. To contemplate this symbol was to engage in meditation upon the Divine. Today many people believe there is a lost knowledge residing in the past, a knowledge that is slowly being rediscovered. The dodecahedron has twelve equilateral pentagon (five-sided) faces and twenty points. The dodecahedron has a connection with the Zodiac and its twelve houses or signs, and when stellated (made into a star) can be related back to the Icosahedron.

Astrology

Another tool that the alchemist used to a far greater degree than we understand today is astrology. In the present day, astrology only survives in tabloid newspapers for most people. Columns of predictions are signposted by headlines such as 'Your Horoscope' while no fairground or seaside pier would be complete without a booth inviting you to find out 'What the Stars Foretell'.

However, just as there is a difference between thaumaturgy and theurgy, so there is a distinct difference between the popular idea of astrology and that used by the alchemists. They would not have considered that they were magicians, but they would have said that they were taking advantage of certain universal conditions which were appropriate for the experiments they were undertaking. In scientific parlance it would today be called 'reducing the variables', for the whole of the Universe was their laboratory.

The Greek scholar and translator Gilbert Murray portrays astrology in something of a bad light when he writes about its invasion of Hellenistic thinking:

> Astrology fell upon the Hellenistic mind as a new disease falls upon some remote island people. The tomb of Ozymandias, as described by Diodorus, was covered with astrological symbols, and that of Antiochus I, which has been discovered in Commagene, is of the same character. It was natural for monarchs to believe that the stars watched over them. But everyone was ready to receive the germ.

Talking about the Stoics, the leading school of Greek philosophy at the time, he went on to write:

> . . . But they were already committed to a belief in the deity

> of the stars and to the doctrine Heimarmenê, or Destiny. They believed in the pervading Pronoia, or Forethought, of the divine mind, and in the Sympathy of all Creation, whereby whatever happens to any one part however remote or insignificant, affects all the rest. It seemed only a natural and beautiful illustration of this Sympathy that the movements of the Stars should be bound up with the sufferings of man.

Gnostic and other older views on astrology, which are much closer to those held by most astrologers today, are summarized in the *Encyclopaedia Britannica (2001)*:

> In the interpretation of Bardesanes, a Syrian Christian scholar – who has often been identified as a Gnostic – the motions of the stars govern only the elemental world, leaving the soul free to choose between the good and the evil. Man's ultimate goal is to attain emancipation from an astrologically dominated material world. Some astrologers, such as the Harranians (from the ancient Mesopotamian city of Harran) and the Hindus, regard the planets themselves as potent deities whose decrees can be changed through supplication and liturgy or through theurgy, the science of persuading the gods or other supernatural powers. In still other interpretations – e.g., that of the Christian Priscillianists (followers of Priscillian, a Spanish ascetic of the 4th century who apparently held dualistic {i.e. Gnostic} views) – the stars merely make manifest the will of God to those trained in astrological symbolism.

It is of course the training and the understanding that are an important factor in the use of the arcane arts such as astrology, sacred geometry and, indeed, theurgy and it is perhaps worth remembering that there was a time when mathematics was seen to be fairly miraculous. Interestingly, with the development of computers, we can again return to some of the ancient ideas about the relationship between mathematics and music and find them provable.

By quoting Irenaeus when he was talking of Marcus who was an avid user of astrology we can perhaps take the arguments in a full circle and accept that there will always be problems in the acceptance of these arts. Iranaeus treats Marcus with his usual contempt and anger:

> Such and other tricks this impostor attempted to perform. And so it was that he was magnified by his dupes, and sometimes he was supposed to utter predictions. But sometimes he tried to make others prophesy, partly by demons carrying on these operations, and partly by practising sleight of hand . . . Hoodwinking therefore multitudes, he led on into enormities, many dupes of this description who had become his disciples by teaching them that they were prone, no doubt, to sin, but beyond the reach of danger, from the fact of their belonging to the perfect power, and of their being participators in the inconceivable potency. And subsequent to the first baptism, to these they promised another which they call Redemption. And by this other baptism they wickedly subvert those that remain with them in expectation of redemption, as if persons, after they had once been baptised, could again obtain remission. Now, it is by means of such knavery as this that they seem to retain their hearers. And when they consider that these have been trusted, and are able to keep secret the mysteries committed unto them, they then admit them to this baptism.

Then, speaking of what would perhaps be called 'channelling' in the present day and also a transference of energy that is perhaps similar to that in the later Cathari *Consulamentum*, he says:

> They, however, do not rest satisfied by this alone, but promise their votaries some other boon for the purpose of confirming them in hope, in order that they may be inseparable adherents of their sect. For they utter something in an inexpressible tone of voice, after having laid hands on him who is receiving the redemption. And they allege that they could not easily declare to another what is thus spoken unless one were highly tested, or one were at the hour of death, when the bishop comes and whispers into the expiring one's ear. And this knavish device is undertaken for the purpose of securing the constant attendance upon the bishop of Marcus' disciples, as individuals eagerly panting to learn what they may be which is spoken at the last, by the knowledge of which the learner will be advanced to the rank of those admitted into the higher mysteries . . .

Iranaeus then really gets into his stride and pooh-poohs Marcus' description of presumably Perfect or Divine Man according to the ancient significances:

> And Marcus alleged that the Quaternion, having explained these things, spoke as follows: 'Now I wish also to exhibit to you Truth herself, for I have brought her down from the mansions above, in order that you may behold here naked, and become acquainted with her beauty; nay also that you may hear her speak, and may marvel at her wisdom. Observe,' says the Quaternion, 'then , first the head above,

Alpha and long O; the neck, B and P; shoulders, along with hands, G and C; breasts, delta and P; diaphragm EU; belly, Z and T; pudenda, Eta and S; thighs, T and R; knees, Ip; calves, Ko; ankles, Lx; feet, M and N.' This is in the body of Truth, according to Marcus. This is the figure of the element; this the character of the letter. And he styles this element Man, and affirms it to be the source of every word, and the originating principle of every sound, and the realisation in speech of everything that is ineffable, and a mouth of taciturn silence . . . I trust, therefore, that as regards these doctrines it is obvious to all possessed of a sound mind, that these tenets are unauthoritative, and far removed from the knowledge that is in accordance with Religion, and are mere portions of astrological discovery, and the arithmetical art of the Pythagoreans.

Spiritual systems

In Chapter Seven we looked at both the Kabbalah and Hermeticism as systems of magic, but we must also look at them as systems of spiritual advancement. These two systems particularly allowed those who could not accustom themselves to the idea of the Good God of the Christians to believe in a more Universal Power. Alchemists were considered heretical in the sense that they were going directly against the given wisdom of the day. Yet to have had the determination and discipline to continue in their experiments against all odds they must also have had perceptions which went beyond the norm.

Above anything else, both the Kabbalah with its Jewish influence and the writings of Thrice Great Hermes with their Egyptian influences could be read in more than one way. In common with all truly great scriptures, the sort of information you drew from it would depend upon your level of understanding. The Gnostics have defined their hierarchy of awareness as:

> Those who carry Sophia's divine spark, the pneumatics
> Those who are psychics, i.e. in touch with the Divine but bound to the soul
> The hylics trapped in matter and probably irredeemable

What was also worthy of note was that the systems of belief tended to surface when they were most needed. They have always been jealously guarded and have only been available or understandable to those who search. When the Kabbalah surfaced in the twelfth century it was at a time of spiritual darkness; when the Hermetic knowledge became available it was as a palliative to oppression and bigotry and only time will tell how the present-day upsurge in interest will manifest.

Far from disappearing, Gnosticism simply went underground. Keith Hopkins regrets what he calls the 'Gnostics' gradual demise':

> Their chaotic inventiveness must have been an ingredient in their failure. They lacked coherence, hierarchy and unified purpose. The sheer virtuosity of their inventions induced more conservative Christians to sharpen the boundaries of orthodoxy. Conservative Christian traditionalists insisted more rigorously on the uniqueness of the single ever-existent Creator and his single human/divine son Jesus. In contrast to the esoteric, mutually conflicting and unverifiable inventions of the Gnostics, conservative Christians also increasingly insisted on a fixed canon of sacred texts, on the bodily resurrection of a historical Jesus, and on the traditions of a 'known' apostolic succession.

Professor Hopkins then contrasts the different perspectives of orthodox Christians and Gnostics:

> Instead of seeking for the divine inside oneself through self-knowledge, orthodox Christians were asked to rely on a professional and hierarchically-ordered priesthood, which claimed an effective monopoly of religious interpretation. Gnostics, by contrast, although they too mostly considered themselves as Christians, were committed to finding a personal redemption by uniting the spirit of the believer with the spirit of the divine. For them, the humanity of Jesus was an embarrassment which could be triumphantly denied. They needed only a spiritual messenger, who could be found and refound in their mythic revelations. The spiritual Jesus, who for Gnostics mattered most, had fought his primal battles before human history had begun.

That the 'demise' was not terminal is seen in the way that Gnosticism persistently resurfaces in each age, if not as given knowledge then certainly as the questions which lead one to the knowledge that is available.

Chapter Nine:

Towards the Present Time

In each new era, one of the questions which tends to be asked is 'What happened to the feminine aspect of God?' Attempts have been made to invest Mary, mother of Jesus, with this aspect but, for a number of people, this has never quite worked since Mary's humanity is insisted upon by the Catholic Church. There is, however, firm evidence that there was a recognizable higher feminine aspect in existence right from the beginning, as can be seen in the Old Testament:

> The Lord possessed me in the beginning of his way, before his works of old. I was set up from everlasting, from the beginning, or ever the earth was. (Proverbs 8: 22–23)

And additionally:

> When he prepared the heavens, I was there: when he set a compass upon the face of the depth: When he established the clouds above: when he strengthened the fountains of the deep: When he gave to the sea his decree, that the waters should not pass his commandment: when he appointed the foundations of the earth: Then was I by him:

> and I was daily his delight, rejoicing always before him. (Proverbs 8: 24–30)

Many of the old alchemists were Gnostics with a strong sense of the religious or mystical who, although they were adept in their craft, were also able to keep their thoughts to themselves.

Jacob Boehme

We have a link between the ancient alchemists and modern thought in Jacob Boehme.

He lived from 1575 to 1624 in Gorlitz, Eastern Germany and, following a mystical experience when he was twenty-five, he became an independent scholar and author while continuing to work as a shoemaker and merchant. Numerous books and tracts on philosophical theology were written by him and his work is still being perused by many today. He was well aware of the fact that he was using alchemical symbolism, particularly in some of the psychological terms in his work. Carl G. Jung frequently refers to Boehme when he is illustrating the dynamics of the psyche's 'alchemical' individuation process: that is, from physical to spiritual. Boehme also seems to have had a profound effect on Jung's religious outlook. In the twentieth century, Alfred North Whitehead developed an advance in religious thinking called process theology, which states that entities are constantly in a process that leads towards becoming something – this also owes a great deal to Boehme.

Boehme's particular brand of mysticism was well-founded in the beliefs of the day. The central idea in his *Lebensphilosophie* (life philosophy) is that reality is a living entity that exists in a state of constant tension between the affirming and suppressing of the possibilities which exist in Unity. In other words, there is a constant dynamic between positive and negative. Those two polarities of 'Yes' and 'No' give one another meaning, that of creating new matter, new form and new definition within that unity.

He accepted that God is immeasurable and cannot be properly defined. At the same time God is process, without beginning or form, a perpetually generating cycle. Interestingly, this has resonance with the Ourobos of the ancients.

Seven kinds of action of Deity were perceived by Boehme, none of which were more important than the others. These were:

1. *Ungrund*, the ungrounded, the hidden Mystery in all things. the transcendent aspect of Being.
2. Primordial Divine Will (*Urwille*), 'Father,' both no-thing (*Nichts*) and everything.
3. Will made subjective, the 'Christ' function.
4. Will made objective, 'Holy Spirit,' movement and life.
5. The Trinity, the coming together or expression of the three Wills giving a creative unity.
6. Logos or 'the Word', the creative vibrational principle, i.e. 'Let there be . . .'
7. Wisdom, Sophia, the feminine principle of God. This acknowledges the androgyny of the Divine from which Trinity and creation are born and exist.

Boehme himself says:

> For I saw and knew the Being of all beings, the ground and the unground; the birth of the holy trinity; the source and origin of this world and all creatures in divine Wisdom (Sophia) . . .
> I saw all three worlds in myself, (1) the divine, angelical, or paradisaical; . . . (2) the dark world . . . ; (3) the external, visible world . . . ; and I saw and knew the whole Being in evil and in good, how one originates in the other . . . so that I not only greatly wondered but also rejoiced.

The central issue apparently running throughout Boehme's work is the thorny question of how God can contain evil. To understand this, he goes beyond the duality of God to the principle of the Eternal One being beyond either – a revolutionary idea in that period. He writes:

> For it cannot be said of God that He is this or that, evil or good, or that He has distinctions in Himself. For He has no tendency to anything, for there is nothing before Him to which He could tend, neither evil nor good. . . . There is no quality or pain in Him . . . [He] is a single will in which the world and the whole creation lies. . . . He is neither light nor darkness, neither love nor wrath, but the Eternal One.

This is a gnostic awareness (knowledge of the Divine), beyond the popular beliefs of the time. Elsewhere he says:

> In this light my spirit directly saw through all things, and knew God in and by all creatures, even in herbs and grass. . . . In this light my will grew in great desire to describe the being of God . . .

Boehme as a mystic has a different perspective on the creation myth and explains it thus:

> The human being is a spirit fashioned as primordial androgynous Adam, image and similitude of Deity. All humans are fundamentally one, whose self-knowledge comes from the one God-man, Adam-Christ. Humans are formed from the Urground in the mirror of Wisdom, as is Trinity itself. Nakedness is the sense of not-belonging in an earth-body.

This, of course, puts a whole different perspective on the idea of carnal knowledge and suggests that, in fact, man remembers his spiritual self; 'his primitive essential unity and his angelical form'. Boehme also recognized the tension between the inner spiritual self and the outer more material being for he says:

> For according to the outward man, we are in this world, and according to the inward man, we are in the inward world . . . Since then we are generated out of both worlds, we speak in two languages, and we must be understood also by two languages.

C.G. Jung

We have already mentioned the effect that Boehme had on Carl Jung's thinking. Jung's perception of the spiritual/physical dynamic and the observation of the tensions between polar opposites in the functions of the psyche (for example, introversion–extraversion, thinking–feeling, sensing–intuiting, masculine–feminine, etc.) is also an illustration of the Boehme idea.

Jung's work on the archetypes arises from his perception of the symbols that man creates for himself. One of the more appealing aspects of Jung's work is his exploration of what he called 'the religious instinct' – that is, the images that rise up from the depths of the psyche, that part of our nature that is totally independent from the conscious mind.

In his later years, Jung was increasingly driven to defend his belief in this viewpoint which he felt gave rise to everything of meaning in art, literature and mythology. In this, he was opposed by Sigmund Freud who argued that this instinct was a sign of infantilism which could be and needed to be 'psychoanalysed out of existence'.

Jung recognized that religious instinct had the power for good or evil, for he was writing very presciently as early as 1916 that:

> As the Christian view loses its authority, the more menacingly will the 'blonde beast' be heard prowling about in its underground prison, ready at any moment to burst out with devastating consequences. When this happens in the individual it brings about a psychological revolution, but it can also take a social form.

Jung recognized that when the personality had no kind of religious authority in place the individual would sense something very raw and untutored within himself, a very basic urge for life which, if not understood and dealt with, could manifest as an aspect of needing to have power over something. This, magnified many times, could lead to problems in society.

Jung also recognized the power of opposites and the fact that such a force has always been present. In a transcription of texts of the Seven Sermons to the Dead purporting to have been written by Basilides in Alexandria he lists them thus:

The Effective and the Ineffective
Fullness and Emptiness
Living and Dead
Difference and Sameness
Light and Darkness
The Hot and the Cold
Force and Matter
Time and Space
Good and Evil
Beauty and Ugliness
The One and the Many

Jung's fascination with the religious component in us is well known. It is based largely on his own personal experiences and emotional responses to them. He warns us that what he expresses in his writings is his own personal viewpoint, but he also says that he also speaks for many people who have had similar experiences. He goes on to say that he does not write as a biblical scholar but merely from his experience as a doctor and an interested party who has had the opportunity to look into the hidden lives of many people.

Just as Jung cannot write in a wholly objective manner in this instance, so we are only able to respond subjectively to his material. We respond from the depth of our own awareness in what might be called a Gnostic fashion.

However, Jeffrey Burke Satinover, past president of the C.G. Jung Foundation, claims that:

> What Jung failed to see was that the awakening of this pagan nature leads inevitably and progressively to Nazi-like phenomena of a greater and greater intensity. To the end of his life he maintained, rather, the Gnostic-like view of things – that an accommodation between 'matter' and 'spirit' could and should be worked out, that the 'dark side' of human nature needed to be integrated into a single, overarching 'wholeness' . . . in its own right truly a modern Gnosticism. It shares with all Gnosticisms a profound blindness to the true nature of evil, a blindness that could be said to arise from its very brilliance.

Dr Satinover acknowledges Jung's gnosticism and continues:

> Jung explicitly identified depth psychology, especially his own, as heir to the Gnostic tradition, especially in what he considered its superiority over Christianity in its handling of the problem of evil.

Further quotes from Jung's later works reveal his closeness to Gnostic thinking. In the chapter 'Christ, a Symbol of the Self', within what is said to be his major work, *Aeon,* he argued that:

> There can be no doubt that the original Christian conception of the imago Dei meant an all-embracing totality that even includes the animal side of man. Nevertheless the Christ-symbol lacks wholeness in the modern psychological sense, since it does not include the dark side of things but it specifically excludes it in the form of a Luciferian opponent.

Jung and the Hermetic Tradition

In developing his system of depth psychology, Jung incorporated certain aspects of the Hermetic tradition. The progressions from Gnosticism and alchemy were seen by him as 'manifestations of unconscious archetypal elements not adequately expressed in the varying forms of Christianity'. He was also 'particularly impressed with his finding that alchemical-like symbols could be found frequently in modern dreams and fantasies'. Also, he saw one of the most important aspects of the individuation process (the journey towards Self) as the union of opposites. This had similar characteristics to the process of *Conjunctio* that is mentioned in ancient texts as the sacred marriage. (see also page XXXX)

Such a union, leading to androgyny, would also account for the Gnostic stories about the love and union between Christ and Sophia (his spiritual mother) and the apparent anomalies which many students of Gnosticism perceive in the creation myths. The unions are 'sacred marriages' in the drive towards Perfection. G.S. Mead makes the point that:

> Hermes . . . is practically one of the very numerous

> permutations and combinations of the Sophia-mythos – one of the many settings-forth of the mystic lore of love of the Christ and the Sophia, or Wisdom, of the Son of God and His spouse or sister, the Holy Spirit, of the King and Queen, of the Lord and the Virgin Church . . . But when we say Gnostic we mean much that is also Hellenic mysticism, and therefore much that is also Hermetic.

Long before Jung, Irenaeus quotes from one Hermetic source:

> 'Prepare thyself as a bride to receive her bridegroom', says Marcus the Gnostic, 'that thou mayest be what I am and I what thou art'.

As we are now familiar with Jung's thinking, we might well find this idea less odd than Irenaeus did. Hermetic thought is all about the union of opposites, but Gilbert Murray was nothing if not cynical about the use that was made of Hermes:

> Originally, outside Homer, Hermes was simply an old upright stone, a pillar furnished with the regular Pelasgian sex-symbol of procreation. Set up over a tomb he is the power that generates new lives, or, in the ancient conception, brings the soul back to be born again. He is the Guide of the Dead, the Psychopompos, the divine Herald between the two worlds.

To put this into context, the Herm was a pillar on which was set a representation of the god Hermes, an androgynous god who was the messenger between two worlds. He was also the guardian of the doorway to one's home, and hence one's boundaries. Murray goes on to say:

> If you have a message for the dead, you speak it to the Herm at the grave. The notion of Hermes as herald may have been helped by his use as a boundary stone – the Latin Terminus. Your boundary stone is your representative, the deliverer of your message, to the hostile neighbour or alien. If you wish to parley with him, you advance up to your boundary stone. If you go, as a Herald, peacefully, into his territory, you place yourself under the protection of the same sacred stone, the last sign that remains of your own safe country. If you are killed or wronged, it is he, the immovable Watcher, who will avenge you.

As Hermes is the messenger between two worlds, the following Hermetic text then falls into place, first as a way of making death acceptable and secondly to show that there are those who will, by their own nature, remain in ignorance:

> 'Hearken, ye folk, men born of earth, who have given yourselves up to drunkenness and sleep in your ignorance of God; awake to soberness, cease to be sodden with strong drink and lulled in sleep devoid of reason.' And when they heard they gathered around me (Hermes) with one accord. And I (Hermes) said, 'O men, why have you given yourself up to death, when you have been granted power to partake of immortality, forsaking corruption.' And some of them mocked at my words, and stand aloof; for they had given themselves up to the way of death. But others besought me that they might be taught, and cast themselves down at my feet. And I bade them stand up; and I made myself a guide to mankind, teaching them the doctrine, how and in what wise they might be saved.

In addition to depth psychology, Jung developed an argument that showed that the 'anti' element of the term 'antichrist' does not mean 'against' but rather 'in the place of'. The emphasis is thus not so much on the figure of a single Antichrist as on the false, specifically Gnostic, representations of Christ that shared certain common characteristics. Chief among these is the presentation of the image of Christ as solely symbolic, mystical or allegorical, thereby returning to a very Docetic idea.Writing of the Gospel of St John, Jung maintains that:

> The coming of the antichrist is not just a prophetic prediction – it is an inexorable psychological law whose existence, though unknown to the author of the Johannine Epistles, brought him a sure knowledge of the impending enantiodromia (the turning of a thing into its opposite). Consequently he wrote as if he were conscious of the inner necessity for this transformation, though we may be sure that the idea seemed to him like a divine revelation. In reality, every intensified differentiation of the Christ-image brings about a corresponding accentuation of its unconscious complement, thereby increasing the tension between above and below.

Contemporary Psychological Thought

Dr Satinover, erstwhile president of the Jung Foundation, denounces the contemporary world for its 'pagan' tendencies – that is, the move towards materialism, amorality and selfish behaviour. In attempting to trace the line between paganism and the present day, he comments on Gnosticism:

> The reappearance of these archaic Gnostic notions in psychological guise, as a fully articulated and widely

> accepted counter-theology, likely reflects both the influence of Jung in divinity schools (where he is commonly and wrong-headedly seen as the only 'spiritual' alternative to a relentlessly triumphant materialism) and the truly astonishing number of clergy who have become Jungian analysts. Many of these are quite prominent both within the churches and within Jungianism. A single historical line thus connects the pagan religions of the ancient Near East (including Canaan), to the Jewish heretical-mystical sects of the Qumran region (the precursors of later Gnosticism, to pre- and early Christian Gnosticism itself, to the Manichean dualism of the late Roman and Aryan empires, to the various classical heresies (Cathar, Albigensian, Bogomil, etc.) to medieval Alchemy and Templarism, and thence into the embracing, transforming alembic of Renaissance Neoplatonism, with its interpenetrating emphases on magic, humanism and science. From here it is but a very short step indeed to the modern reduction of spirit to psyche and/or soma and the consequent pagan resurgence through which we are now suffering.

Presumably, recognizing that meaninglessness, or in psychological terms, anomie, causes huge problems, he continues:

> In reaction to the profound reductionism latent in the classical psychoanalytic vision of man, explicitly spiritual schools of psychoanalysis and psychology have arisen, largely influenced by Jung, that directly embrace the pagan, Gnostic solution to the dread of meaninglessness, taking the instincts themselves, and spiritualising them to fill the void. Yet here, too, in this seemingly opposite approach, man's merely animal nature is vaulted once again in the highest place of honour.

Some scholars and theologians would see such spiritualization as a counterbalance to the secularization of society and would say that it proves the existence of some kind of religious imperative.

In an article written in 1995, Robert A. Segal, an academic theologian, refuted Satinover's arguments by saying that:

> Gnosticism is now often taken as an ancient religion in its own right . . . The aim is to terminate any connection between immateriality and matter.

He expands on this by pointing out that:

> . . . In applying the term to current developments contemporary thinkers identify Gnosticism with the belief that human beings are alienated either from their true selves or from the world. Neither the true self nor the world need be immaterial. Indeed, there need be no fixed self or any world beyond the material one. There certainly need be no god. Contemporary Gnosticism apparently need not even involve the cosmos. The dualism can be between parts of the personality, between nations or between classes. The dualism need not even be antagonistic. The thinkers most credited with the application of the label 'Gnostic' to modernity have paralleled but not equated the ancient outlook with the modern one. They have often been concerned with the differences as well as the similarities between the two.

Segal brings us up to date with modern thinking very neatly when he puts forward another philosopher's viewpoint:

> The philosopher Hans Jonas was the first to compare

> ancient Gnosticism with modern existentialism. (Gnosticism and Modern Nihilism, 1952) For Jonas, the central tenet of both is the entrapment of human beings in a world at odds with their true nature. Jonas emphasises that the two outlooks are far from identical. In Gnosticism the world is demonic and hostile; in existentialism it is impersonal and indifferent. In Gnosticism one is presently separated from one's true self; in existentialism one has no fixed nature. In Gnosticism the alienation is surmountable; in existentialism it is not.

The political philosopher Eric Voegelin (1901–1985) used the term Gnosticism to condemn modernity. He put forward the theory that modern individuals and movements have six characteristics that identify what he calls 'the Gnostic attitude':

1. Dissatisfaction with the world
2. Confidence that the wrongs in the world arise from the way it is organized
3. Certainty that amelioration is possible
4. The assumption that improvement must 'evolve historically'
5. The belief that human beings can change the world
6. The conviction that knowledge – *gnosis* – is the key to change

As time goes on, it can be seen that Mankind is 'in process'. As the various strands of religion (belief) *gnosis* (knowledge) and emotion (feeling) are brought together, a much more coherent whole emerges. Segal says:

> . . . Whereas Voegelin uses the term 'Gnostic' negatively, Jung uses it positively. Like Jonas, Jung merely compares, rather than identifies, Gnosticism with modernity. But

> whereas for Jonas the chief similarity between Gnosticism and modernity is 'alienation from the world', for Jung it is alienation from oneself . . . Jung applauds Gnostics as budding Jungians. The hidden spark which they seek is really the unconscious. In their dissatisfaction with their present lives, their quest for something more, and their joyful discovery of a self from which they have been severed, Gnostics are akin to Jungians, and psychology is the modern counterpart of ancient Gnosticism.

So, in the present day, we consider that the search for self is all-important. Psychology is perhaps the modern counterpart of Gnosticism, but if the latter is to survive it must grow and change. Just as the ancient gnostics had their various sects, practices and viewpoints, so modern day Gnosticism has to ensure that it remains broad-minded and open to change. It must incorporate old ideas – Hellenistic, Pagan Christian and ethnic. It must learn from its own mythology and adapt and rectify.

Old stories that were suitable for a simpler people can be modified in the light of present-day knowledge. Gnosticism can become a message of hope and creativity for the future instead of being a source of gloom and despondency.

In *On the Nature of the Psyche*, Jung writes:

> Since psyche and matter are contained in one and the same world, and moreover are contained in continuous contact with one another and ultimately rest on irrepresentable, transcendental factors, it is not only possible but fairly probable, even, that psyche and matter are two different aspects of one and the same thing.

Docetists

For the moment, let us concentrate briefly on the Docetists, for they offer a good example of how, with the right timing, an idea can catch on and survive. The central argument of the Docetists is that the figure on the cross was not a real man but a phantom that emerged immediately after the crucifixion – an idea that rumbles on. In the light of the knowledge that the etheric or astral body is a measurable force and that clairvoyants are capable of seeing the spirit depart the body at death, this is not so strange.

Even St Paul might have believed in such a theory, judging by his observation that there are many kinds of bodies. St John must also have been concerned about something close to home when he said 'many deceivers are entered into the world who confess not that Jesus Christ is come in the flesh'. (II John 1: 7) The continuing importance of docetism lies not so much in its relevance as a piece of antique folklore, but in its effect on our understanding of the meaning of Resurrection.

The Christian dogma of physical resurrection presupposes that the body of Jesus was real. However, such a belief is so opposed to common sense that it apparently conflicts with arguments for survival after death. It is easy to see how such an unnecessary or unbearable contradiction must have driven people away from the church.

Hastings' *Encyclopaedia of Religion and Ethics* (Vol. IV. 833) is clear in its support for the various types of Docetism:

> There are traces of Docetism in several apocryphal books that circulated for a time among early Christians. We have seen that Serapion of Antioch forbade the reading of the Gospel of Peter because it had been corrupted by Docetes . . . The Acts of John (early 2nd cent.; cf. Euseb. HE iii. 25) exhibits the most pronounced form. At the Last Supper, St

> John, leaning on Christ's breast, found it non-resisting (89, Hennecke, NT Apokryphen, Tubingen, 1904, p. 451); at the entombment, the body of Christ was at one moment apparently solid, at another it was 'it was immaterial and incorporeal and like nothing' (93 ib. 452). The Crucifixion was only an appearance; at the same moment Christ appeared to John on the Mount of Olives and explained this (97 ib. 454).

In essence, the Docetic belief seems to be very close to the teachings of Eastern religions on the subject of the body being capable of refining itself to the point where it becomes a 'Being of Light' and therefore immortal. Taking into account the fact that many Gnostics believe that Jesus Christ was Divine Man, such a belief would seem to be entirely feasible.

Nevertheless, orthodox Christians who believe in bodily resurrection lean heavily on Job's statement that 'though after my skin the worms destroy this body, yet in my flesh shall I see God . . .' (Job 19: 26). These words have recently been reinterpreted in the new Standard Revised Version ' . . . after my skin has been thus destroyed, then without my flesh I shall see God.' This suggests that the soul lives on even though the physical body has been destroyed.

Modern Writers

When we consider modern figures within gnosticism we perhaps have to differentiate between those who adhere to a frankly Gnostic viewpoint, those who acknowledge the influence of Gnosticism and those who do not see Gnosticism as playing any part at all in the thought of today. In the rest of this chapter, a brief look is taken at several well-known modern writers on Gnosticism.

Elaine Pagels has carried out a great deal of research on material from the Nag Hammadi texts. According to *Encyclopedia Britannica* (2001) she is one of

> only a few academics read by both their peers and the general public . . . Her exploration of the documents exploded the myth of a solid unity within the early Christian movement and also explored the feminine imagery and ideology present in the Gnostic texts.

She has written a number of books on Gnosticism. The best-known of these is perhaps *The Gnostic Gospels*. In an on-line review of her book it is stated that:

> One initially feels in The Gnostic Gospels that Pagels is writing as an apologist for the gnostics. The effect of the whole, however, is one of impartial weighing and sifting rather than proselytizing for a resurrected gnosticism. Pagels' arguments come full course when she acknowledges that Christianity may very well not have survived were it not for the political acumen of the orthodox bishops, those same bishops, moreover, who saw it as their duty to crush the gnostic movement.

This is followed by an extract from *The Gnostic Gospels*:

> Had Christianity remained multiform [i.e. had it continued to include a variety of gnostic communities in addition to the orthodox community], it might well have disappeared from history, along with dozens of rival religious cults of antiquity. I believe that we owe the survival of Christian tradition to the organizational and theological structure that the emerging church developed. Anyone as powerfully

> attracted to Christianity as I am will regard that as a major achievement.

Harold Bloom has written several books with gnosticism as the theme. After having undertaken much study, Bloom rejects New Ageism in favour of Gnosticism. In a review of *Omens of the Millenium (1996)*, Professor Lee Irwin comments:

> Bloom's strategy is to relocate the nexus of spiritual growth and development in the 'self' and not in any institutionalized, dogmatic religion, an attitude he claims is reflected by popular interests in the paranormal and the apocalyptic. While 'Bloom does not wish to worship Bloom' (p. 17), he repudiates the superficial self-interests of much New Age spirituality which he sees as a mix of 'occultism and American harmonial faith suspended about half way between feeling good and good feeling' (p. 19). The search for transcendence as he sees it requires the seeker to move beyond both the material universe and the empirical, everyday self into the indwelling divine source of immortality. This is not a matter of faith but of knowledge (gnosis), of knowing and of being known, of seeing the divine spark within, even in the fallen condition of incarnate life. He strongly emphasizes this element of the 'estrangement or even alienation of God' (p. 27) who abandons the cosmos while leaving the spark of divinity in every person. For Bloom, gnosticism arises as a 'protest' against failed apocalypticism, as a consequence of resistance to the ever-turning wheel of historical becoming.

In a review of Stuart Holroyd's *Elements of Gnosticism*, Eric Mader-Lin writes that it is 'a book that sets out to present the teachings of the ancient Gnostics and to trace the legacy of their beliefs over the centuries'.

> As far as the first of these goals is concerned, namely his presentation of the major Gnostic doctrines and movements, the book is worth reading. It is only when Holroyd sets his sights on finding Gnostic thought in post-medieval Western society that he becomes markedly less convincing. In these latter chapters, he is usually reduced to exploiting as best he can any thematic parallels he can discover between ancient Gnostic texts and the major works of such writers as Goethe, Melville and Sartre.

Chapter Ten:

Gnostics and Gnosticism Today

When looking at Gnosticism the general consensus of opinion seems to be that what started as a radical way of looking at, and perhaps explaining, life in the pre-Christian era has survived the vicissitudes of the years and is still able to play a valid part in the life of today. Interestingly, Gnosticism is perhaps just as radical now as it ever was. Buckminster Fuller (1895–1983), who was probably one of the twentieth century's more radical thinkers, poses a meaningful question:

> If we can find nature's own coordinate system, we might really be able to bring together the chasm between the humanists and the scientists. THAT'S THE VERY ESSENCE OF ALL THE THINGS I'M COMMUNICATING TO YOU ALL HERE. Is there a structure common to both physical and metaphysical reality?

As we saw earlier, 'Gnosis' means knowledge through experience and 'ism' is defined as a distinctive doctrinal system or theory, so we might define Gnosticism as a distinctive theory of special knowledge. Looked at in that way, perhaps there *is* a structure that is common to both metaphysical and physical reality – Gnosticism, in fact. This immediately catapaults us into all the arguments both for and against the 'religion' of Gnosticism, but it does not really provide us with an answer.

If God were wholly good how could he create a world such as ours? On the other hand, if he were wholly bad then what was the payoff in his creation? It is only when we move away from the idea of religion and get back to the idea of Gnostic thought that we can see how everything ties in together – and how it applies to the present day.

Briefly, if we look again at the myths of Gnosticism we can remind ourselves that they were tales told to explain certain phenomena. There are many myths, but they all have a central theme:

> Gnostics believed in the distinction between spirit and matter, the one good and the other evil. They were dualists, although some would reconcile dualism with primitive monism. To all of them, God, pure spirit and supreme good, could have no direct contact with matter and the creation of this present evil world. They provided, therefore, for a succession of emanations from him. It was through the demiurge or creator, one of the more remote of these emanations, or aeons, that the world came into existence by a bridging of the gap between spirit and matter. Into this world were introduced by a higher aeon sparks of divinity which found lodgment in human beings. The problem for men equipped with this spark was to be freed from contamination with matter and to be restored to the realm of pure spirit. Not all men had this spark of divinity, but even if they possessed it they could not save themselves. That must be done by God. This saving work of God had been performed by Christ, whom the Gnostics identified with one of the aeons.

Stephan Hoeller, who is the founder of the Gnostic Society in America, makes the point that:

> To what extent various Gnostics took these mythologies literally is difficult to discern. What is certain is that behind the myths there are important metaphysical postulates which have not lost their relevance. The personal creator who appears in Genesis does not possess the characteristics of the ultimate, transcendental 'ground of being' of which mystics of many religions speak. If the God of Genesis has any reality at all, it must be a severely limited reality, one characterized by at least some measure of foolishness and blindness. While the concept of two Gods is horrifying to the monotheistically conditioned mind, it is not illogical or improbable. Modern theologians, particularly Paul Tillich, have boldly referred to 'the God above God'. Tillich introduced the term 'ground of being' as alternative language to express the divine. The ideas of the old Gnostics seem not so outdated after all.

Elsewhere he writes:

> The noted scholar of Gnosticism, G. Filoramo, wrote:
> Jung's reflections had long been immersed in the thought of the ancient Gnostics to such an extent that he considered them the virtual discoverers of 'depth psychology' . . . ancient Gnosis, albeit in its form of universal religion, in a certain sense prefigured, and at the same time helped to clarify, the nature of Jungian spiritual therapy.
>
> In the light of such recognitions one may ask: 'Is Gnosticism a religion or a psychology?' The answer is that it may very well be both. Most mythologems found in

> Gnostic scriptures possess psychological relevance and applicability. For instance the blind and arrogant creator-demiurge bears a close resemblance to the alienated human ego that has lost contact with the ontological self. Also, the myth of Sophia resembles closely the story of the human psyche that loses its connection with the collective unconscious and needs to be rescued by the Self. Analogies of this sort exist in great profusion.

Claude Levi-Strauss (born 1908) is a social anthropologist who propounds the idea that cultures, among which he included Gnosticism, were 'systems of communication'. He constructed models involving linguistics, information theory and cybernetics to interpret them. Among his many works, the one that is most significant in this context is his four-volume analysis of myths: *The Raw and the Cooked (1964)*; *From Honey to Ashes (1966)*; *The Origin of Table Manners (1968)*; and *The Naked Man (1971)*. In this structuralist study he observes that cultural relations appear as pairs of opposites. He is interested in why myths from different cultures are often similar, given that their content could be anything and everything that suits the spiritual needs of the people at that time. He suggests that myths:

> provide a logical model capable of overcoming a contradiction such as how can a wholly good Supreme Being result in a world that contains evil?

Let us look, therefore, for an understanding of the creation of True Father and the Demiurge.

The True Father and the Demiurge

Within the *Apocryphon of John*, a Gnostic text, there is a myth that can be easily deconstructed so that the structure can be found and the logical model discovered. The main focus of the story is pre-creation, for great care is taken to name many of the beings created by Yaldabaoth and to explain the nature of the universe before the creation of the physical world. Adam and Eve's difficulties are also discussed and 'for those who have ears to hear' it provides a matrix for life within the world.

Before the material world came into existence, according to this text, there was Light:

> He is immeasurable light, which is pure, holy (and) immaculate. He is ineffable, being perfect in incorruptibility. (He is) not in perfection, nor in blessedness, nor in divinity, but he is far superior. He is not corporeal nor is he incorporeal. He is neither large nor is he small. There is no way to say, 'What is his quantity?' or, 'What is his quality?', for no one can know him.

From Light there came a series of Emanations, non-corporeal cosmic beings in male–female pairs. Within the Light itself there were three especially important beings: the Father, the Mother and the Son. Beneath the trinity, there is a kind of creative 'soup' consisting of Water, Darkness, the Abyss, and Chaos (four common elements of many pre-creation stories) within which the trinity exists.

One of the Emanations, Sophia, decides to create life without uniting with her masculine counterpart and the result is a deformed god named Yaldabaoth, the demiurge:

> And the Sophia of the Epinoia, being an aeon, conceived a thought from herself and the conception of the invisible Spirit and foreknowledge. She wanted to bring forth a likeness out of herself without the consent of the Spirit, –

> he had not approved – and without her consort, and without his consideration. And though the person of her maleness had not approved, and she had not found her agreement, and she had thought without the consent of the Spirit and the knowledge of her agreement, (yet) she brought forth.

In his arrogance, Yaldeboath decides that he is the most powerful being in the universe and he declares himself to be the only God. The demiurge then goes on to create the physical world, together with various archons, heavens and powers. Some of these are thought to belong to the 365 days of the year and others to the seven days of the week. Yet others seem to be more personal, for they deal with emotional and mystic forces.

The Apocryphon is incredibly detailed as to the creation of man. The Archons, as we have seen elsewhere, attempt to create a man. They fail to give him life, however, since they cannot make him move until Sophia tricks Yaldeboath into breathing his essence of the Light into man, allowing him to become a living being. Finally comes the creation story of Genesis with its episode in the garden: Adam and Eve eat of the 'Tree of Knowledge' and are cast out.

It is an interesting exercise to deconstruct the myth simply in an effort to understand the culture and thinking which gave birth to it. It is possible to read all sorts of significances into it, particularly on an intuitive level: perhaps with a sense of shock. Many of these significances are valid in the present day.

First we have Unity in the Light; then duality in the pairing; recognition of the Three in the Trinity; four within the creative soup and so on. If we allow it to, this can take us into the hidden significance of number while it enables us to understand the thinking of Pythogoras and his peers.

Looked at from a Jungian perspective, we can see the main points of

Depth psychology. The higher self (Sophia) seeks expression, and man – ultimately her responsibility – moves from dependency to autonomy. If we wish, we can venture further into an understanding of personal relationships and, following the model of the myth, we can discover how we can come to terms with our own inner urges and desires.

Because we need not be constrained by cultural teachings, we can explore the Gnostic beliefs in the search for the spiritual self, thereby opening ourselves up to experiences which would otherwise be denied to us. While some of the ideas may seem strange, they require us to suspend disbelief and to try and approach the whole question with an open mind and with the simplicity of the early Gnostics. By doing so, we are actually able to put ourselves in touch with a very basic primeval energy which brings fresh knowledge.

A New Perspective

If the Nag Hammadi texts had not been discovered, it is more than probable that the current renewal of interest in Gnosticism would not have taken place. There will always be those who do not see eye to eye with mainstream ideas, so it is highly unlikely that Gnostic thought would have died out altogether. However, the texts that were found gave new impetus to research into the early Gnostics and their system of belief. Not only the academics but also young people who were perhaps overly conscious of the results of war – which had after all been worldwide – were given an opportunity to focus on something other than death and destruction.

The perennial questions of life, some of which we have highlighted previously, needed answering – 'How could a good God . . .? What if for instance . . . an A-bomb does destroy? Where do you go when you are dead?' When this was added to the existence of a new freedom, both financial and moral, there was a need for a different way of thinking. Strangely enough, without putting a name to it, one of the core beliefs belonging to Gnosticism became more prevalent. The only hope for humanity was to acquire the information it needed so that it could perfect itself and evolve out of its current physical state.

New Age thought began to develop and people began to realize that the main problem within the world was that we had let the knowledge of our own Christ consciousness pass us by. When we rekindled that light within us, according to Joseph Campbell, it would be the very essence of Christian Gnosticism and the Thomas Gospel.

Much of Gnostic thought, therefore, was being incorporated into New Age beliefs – partly because it was so close to the main principles of the Eastern religions and partly, if we are totally honest, because people with Christian ideals did not have to move too far away from their own base. They could explore new ways of thinking in the name of research.

At the same time, the new science of sociology was becoming better understood, so its methods could be applied to a culture in order to discover how groups of people had handled new information and innovative groupings. The dynamics of a group such as the disciples and their charismatic leader – whether he was divine or otherwise – provided a model for understanding the psychology behind the way in which people might get together in order to practise new ways of being. The return to pagan ways of thought worked for many, but for others there needed to be something different.

With the translation of some of the Gnostic texts into English the world had access to material that had formed the thought of the early Christian Gnostics. It offered alternative, perhaps pure, sources that were not coloured by the invective of the orthodox Christians.

We can speculate at length as to whether the texts are genuine or simply copies of the then existing gospels. The fact of the matter is that they offer a different viewpoint. The Gnostic Jesus, far from dying as an atonement for the sins of the world, an act that many might think was pointless, actually descended from the spiritual realm in order to make information available that was necessary both for self-perfection and for the perfection of the whole human race.

Feminists and the Emancipation of the Feminine

From a global perspective there were other things happening at around that time. Whether one took the pragmatic approach or looked for a more mystical reason would depend on one's own system of belief.

There was a point following the death of John F. Kennedy at which it seemed that women took a collective deep breath and refused to continue to condone the death and destruction that was occurring around them. Whether it was the invention of the contraceptive pill that gave women more freedom or a call from Sophia in her guise of redeemer is immaterial – and perhaps the two are linked anyway. This is perfectly expressed in an excerpt from one of the texts.

> Hear me, you hearers
> and learn of my words, you who know me.
> I am the hearing that is attainable to everything;
> I am the speech that cannot be grasped.
> I am the name of the sound
> and the sound of the name.
> I am the sign of the letter
> and the designation of the division.

An imperative to look beyond the self was there and women began to look for role models and to develop a worship and appreciation of not just the personalization of the Goddess but of Sophia as Feminine Wisdom. All of this represented the Gnostic voice from a past before – as Elaine Pagels says – virtually all the feminine imagery for God had disappeared from orthodox Christian tradition

Orthodox opinion echoed Tertullian's exclamation from centuries before:

> These heretical women – how audacious they are! They have no modesty; they are bold enough to teach, to engage in argument, to enact exorcisms, to undertake cures, and, it may be, even to baptise.

In trying to give some structure to the new orthodox church, St Paul had stated categorically that:

> It is not permitted for a woman to speak in the church, nor is it permitted for her to teach, nor to baptise, nor to offer (the eucharist), nor to claim for herself a share in any masculine function – not to mention any priestly office.

Yet it is quite plain from the Nag Hammadi texts that far from being suppressed women did have their rightful place and that the inherent strength of woman was recognized.

> While her enemies look at her in shame, she runs upward into her treasure-house – the one in which her mind is – and (into) her storehouse which is secure, since nothing among the things that have come into being has seized her, nor has she received a stranger into her house. For many are her homeborn ones who fight against her by day and by night, having no rest by day or by night, for their lust oppresses them.

So, in a way, the decision of the Church of England Synod to approve the ordination of women in the present day is a reversion to Gnostic attitudes and women's transmission of knowledge. In the *Gospel of Thomas*, Peter was perhaps jealous of the attention that Mary was getting, for he asks Jesus to make her go away because 'women are not worthy of life'. In recognition of the development of Mary's inner strength, and her ability to move through and beyond her own 'femaleness', Jesus says, almost in reproach:

> Look, I will draw her in so as to make her male, so that she too may become a living male spirit, similar to you. (But I say to you): 'Every women who makes herself male will enter the kingdom of heaven.

Karen King, Professor of New Testament studies and the history of ancient Christianity at Harvard University comes to the conclusion that the Gnostic texts are not helpful in the growth of feminism. In *Images of the Feminine in Gnosticism,* a book that she has edited, King makes the observation that:

> It seems to me that even when the feminine is highly valued, it is often done so at the expense of real sexuality. It also seems as though gnostic mythology and gender imagery often affirm patriarchy and patriarchal social gender roles.

She also elsewhere states:

> Gnostic myth can be seen as a response within Mediterranean society to changing social circumstances . . . Gnostic myth makers are shaping their stories out of their own cultures' traditions, which could be pagan, Jewish, Egyptian, Christian or even Gnostic given the degree of individualism among local thinkers.

The Demiurge Today

Those who wish to understand the meaning of the creation of evil can also find significance in Gnostic attitudes. Many feminists today are disturbed at the way that womankind is blamed for the Fall within the Garden of Eden – the episode in which the serpent tempted Eve who then made her husband eat of the Tree of Knowledge.

Gnostic myth gives a slightly different twist to this story. Rather than it being Eve who makes the mistake it is actually Sophia; and she must do everything that she can to put it right. She has attempted an emanation – a projection beyond herself which is flawed, without the support of her natural polarity, and which takes on a life and power of its own: which then goes out of control. She must now deal with this emanation, containing and taming it with the help of the other aeons – they all join together in a kind of mass effort.

At the same time she must unite with the Logos, her proper counterpart, if there is to be a proper correction – and a gathering in of all the aspects of herself which have become scattered. She must also have her own creation recognize the error of his ways – that is that evil leads to evil. Whether we choose to look at this from a mythological or a psychological point of view, it behoves us to learn from Sophia's mistakes in the present day. That is, we should not to try to create from a unilateral perspective and we should collaborate rather than co-operate. Women must also take responsibility for their mistakes. In plain terms, women in particular must realize that they cannot act without consultation – it is the combination or androgyny of Wisdom and Logic that can effect change and turn the principle of wisdom into knowledge. Truly a Gnostic idea.

Androgyny

The idea of two forces – opposites or polarities – coming together is an idea that permeates most religions which are not wholly monotheistic. For Gnosticism in particular, the union of opposites comes up over and over again. As we have seen, emanations that are essentially balanced emerge from the union between God and his Protonnoia. Some instances of where balance is needed are: First Man is the union of two fires the light and the dark; Adam must find his partner; and the physical world is evil and the spiritual world is good but they must be brought together. All these ideas demonstrate that out of duality must come unity. This union or marriage is now becoming evident in very subtle ways in today's world. Jung and his followers uncovered some of the hidden meanings in the translations of the Gnostic texts and the world is richer for it. In bringing about an understanding of the hidden feminine in the masculine, and vice versa, androgyny has allowed freedom of expression in a way that has not been feasible in other eras. It is no longer considered odd if a man openly expresses his more sensitive side or a woman uses her energy in drive and power.

The extension of this is that people are becoming more aware of their spiritual selves. David Bowie, possibly one of the arch exponents of androgyny in his early days, summed up his position when he married in 1992:

> I'm not a religious person. I'm a spiritual person. God plays a very important part in my life – I look to Him a lot and He is the cornerstone of my existence. . . I believe man develops a relationship with his own God . . . Religion is for people who believe in hell; spirituality is for people who've been there.

The idea of being trapped in some alternative reality and needing to escape is one of the ideas central to Gnostic belief. Bowie shows a perhaps unconscious Gnosticism in his Ziggy Stardust character. A scholar of rock says:

> In Bowie's visionary performance, the story went that

> civilisation was going to collapse and the 'Infinites' would arrive. Ziggy Stardust (a sort of a Golem, 'your face, your race, the way that you talk/I kiss you, you're beautiful, I want you to walk') was advised to announce the coming of these 'starmen' bringing hope. Ziggy is their prophet, the messiah who takes himself to incredible spiritual heights, and is kept alive by the devotion of his disciples. When the 'starmen' finally arrive, they take bits and pieces of Ziggy so that they can manifest themselves as real physical beings. Eventually they tear him to pieces on stage during the performance of the song Rock'n'Roll Suicide. At the moment of Ziggy's death, the 'starmen' take on his essence, and become visible. The drama is gnosticism at its purest. In Manicheism, every man and woman were once stars, that is divine. Through a Philip K. Dick-like 'crack in the sky', most of the divine quality reascended to heaven, leaving behind only some tiny little sparks of the Divine Light.

Androgyny also presents itself in a rather odd way in the present day. Women have realized that they are powerful in their own right, but that they also have to learn not to abuse that power. Gnostic texts in the early Christian era do give women their rightful place in the scheme of things but in the modern day they must also appreciate that they should not emasculate their menfolk. There is a distinct danger that men can be reduced to quivering impotency – a state akin to the Gnostic Adam. In one of the myths it was Sophia's function to have Adam stand upright. Eve is perceived as Sophia's daughter and was able to help Adam to do this.

More modern-day Gnostic practices

There are two further aspects of modern living in relation to

Gnosticism which are worth highlighting. A rise in vegetarianism and veganism has been noted over the last two decades. The majority of those who adopt this way of life usually do so from a religious perspective. This often owes a great deal to the rise of Eastern religions and the reverence for life.

However, as we have seen, there was a branch of Gnosticism which accepted vegetarianism for a different reason. The Cathari and others would not eat the flesh of animals lest it was contaminated by the necessary copulation that was involved in reproduction. They recognized – without putting it in so many words – that in order to achieve perfection of spirit they must not contaminate their own flesh. A version of this thinking is pertinent in the present day, for we receive many contaminants from the environment and we should probably attempt to make ourselves as 'pure' as possible in order to attain our highest state of consciousness or awareness. Choosing to be vegetarian might be a step towards escaping from the grossness of the present-day world and a move towards a different perception of the life we live and the cosmos in which we do it.

Rave Culture

The other side of the coin is, of course, what has popularly been called the Rave Culture. Broadly speaking, this would seem at first glance to be a deliberate contamination of one's own being through drugs and excess and yet in its own parlance it is an attempt to be 'out of it' – to induce a purposeful change of consciousness. In essence, the Rave Culture is no different to the Dionysian rites we saw earlier in the book, which were a way of leaving the mundanity of the everyday world behind and achieving, for a short time, a change of consciousness through rhythm and dance.

Such changes can be extremely harmful when carried to excess, for they can lead to misperceptions and hallucinations. When it is understood that a chemically induced change is seldom as successful as a naturally induced one, we can then move away from a slightly primitive method to a more sophisticated awareness. In Gnostic terms we move from a hyalic bodily reaction to a more psychic (soul) response. It can be the beginning of the awakening of the Divine spark (the *pneuma*).

Back to the Beginning

So who would want to admit to being a Gnostic today? Because there is more religious freedom there is necessarily less overt persecution – yet when there is less comprehension there is less acceptance and few people today have a real understanding of what Gnosticism is. No Gnostic would now be accused of heresy, although they might possibly be accused of anarchy. Present-day Gnostic organizations differ greatly from the sects of the early days and yet just as many ideas and beliefs can be put under the umbrella of Gnosticism.

Interest in Gnosticism surged during the postwar years. Gnostic institutions of a scholarly or religious kind, catering for a generation of young people with no taste for orthodoxy, were spawned in the midst of mysterious, mystical, occult, 'new age', anti-establishment outlooks. In the 1950s, Richard, Duc de Palatine established the Order of the Pleroma in England and he sent Stephan A. Hoeller to the US to spread the message. They separated in the 1970s, whereupon Hoeller started the Gnostic Society and a church, the Ecclesia Gnostica, which uses Catholic ceremonies and vestments but Gnostic language and the Gospels of Sophia and Thomas. He provides an interesting view of Gnosticism as

> . . . an experience that does not lend itself to the language of theology of philosophy, but which is instead closely affinitized to, and expresses itself through the medium of

> myth . . . the term 'myth' should not here be taken to mean 'stories that are not true' but rather that the truths embodied in these myths are of a different order from the dogmas of theology or the statements of philosophy.

He goes on to say that:

> Like Buddhism, Gnosticism begins with the fundamental recognition that earthly life is filled with suffering and that many religions advocate that humans are to be blamed for the imperfections of the world . . . Gnostics respond that this interpretation of the myth is false. The blame for the world's failings lies not with humans but with the creator . . . The Gnostic God concept is more subtle than that of most religions. In its way it unites and reconciles the recognitions of Monotheism and Polytheism, as well as Theism, Deism and Pantheism.

As for long-suffering people:

> Humans are generally ignorant of the divine spark resident within them. This ignorance is fostered in human nature by the influence of the false creator and his Archons . . . Not all humans are spiritual (pneumatics) and thus ready for Gnosis and liberation . . . Gnostics do not look to salvation from sin (original or other), but rather from the ignorance of which sin is a consequence. Ignorance – whereby is meant ignorance of spiritual realities – is dispelled only by Gnosis.

And as a terminal, downbeat observation:

> Death does not automatically bring about liberation from bondage in the realms of the Demiurge . . . Gnosticism does not emphasise the doctrine of reincarnation prominently, but it is implicitly understood in most Gnostic teachings that those who have not made effective contact with their transcendental origins while they were in embodiment would have to return into the sorrowful condition of earthly life.

Other churches include The American Gnostic Church in Texas, set up in 1985, which follows the teaching of Basilides, and The Ecclesia Gnostica Mysteriorum, which was set up in Palo Alto. In 1984, the Lumen Foundation was founded for the purpose of providing instruction in the fields of Western philosophy and esoteric, mystical and spiritual traditions through publications, lectures or otherwise. Educational material was also disseminated by the Foundation. Another aim was to provide a public forum for the discussion of such matters – primarily through, but not limited to, the medium of print. Its founders' pride and joy was a journal called *Gnosis Magazine*. It has since run out of money, but its 'gnosis' is still available in a Penguin/Arkana paperback, *Hidden Wisdom*, edited by former editors of *Gnosis*. The Gnostic Apostolic Church, based in Australia has an extremely comprehensive online booklet which explains and clarifies many Gnostic ideas.

Conclusion

The title of this book is *The Essence of the Gnostics*. Let us now 'gather up the sparks', as it were, and put everything into perspective so that we can decide if we are now clear about the nature of Gnostics and Gnosticism. We defined Mystery religions in Chapter Two, so we might look to see if Gnosticism qualifies as such a religion.

- There is often an initiation ceremony which is some form of cleansing process . . . Even in early times, the initiate had to be introduced by other members. By recognizing his feminine aspect, God was introduced to himself.
- Adherents to the belief take part in a ritual meal on a regular basis . . . Transubstantiation is often a feature of those meals, when a mundane substance takes on a highly religious or esoteric significance.

  The process of creation was the opposite of this in that the Divine took on a mundane form.
- The birth and death of the instigator of the religion is in some way miraculous or remarkable.

  There was no birth and there has been no death, for the prime motivator of the religion is Pure Light or Divinity itself.

- At death, or on what appears to be death, he is restored to life but he ultimately ends up in heaven, thus proving his divinity.
  Since this Light is never ending it constantly restores itself and is pictured as doing so in the form of the Ourobos.
- The female principle or Divine Mother image is often very strong. Sometimes she is depicted as Mother Earth or as a Consort, but she is always given her rightful place as Progenitor.
  Sophia is constantly depicted as the Divine Mother, particularly in her care for the results of her own creation.
- Whilst he is living, the divine man is often ridiculed but he takes care to impart certain arcane knowledge to his followers.
  Gnosticism is based on the need to know and understand God.

Now it could be said that it is stretching credulity to call gnosticism a mystery religion but it is certainly a religion of Mysteries – all those things about which everyone wonders. Gnosticism makes an attempt to answer our questions about the origin of God and once we go behind the myths we are left with one overriding question. How did the Ineffable Pure Light become? Rather than go in that direction let Sophia have the last word in a hymn of praise that is included in *The Nag Hammadi Library*:

> I was sent forth from (the) power,
> and I have come to those who reflect upon me,
> and I have been found among those who seek after me.
> Look upon me, you who reflect upon me,
> and you hearers, hear me.
> You who are waiting for me, take me to yourselves.
> And do not banish me from your sight.
> And do not make your voice hate me, nor your hearing.
> Do not be ignorant of me anywhere or any time. Be on
> your guard!

Do not be ignorant of me.
For I am the first and the last,
I am the honoured one and the scorned one,
I am the whore and the holy one.
I am the wife and the virgin.
I am the (mother) and the daughter.
I am the members of my mother.
I am the barren one
and many are her sons.
I am she whose wedding is great,
and I have not taken a husband.
I am the midwife and she who does not bear.
I am the solace of my labour pains.
I am the bride and the bridegroom,
and it is my husband who begot me.
I am the mother of my father
and the sister of my husband,
and he is my offspring.
I am the silence that is incomprehensible
and the idea whose remembrance is frequent.
I am the voice whose sound is manifold
and the word whose appearance is multiple
I am the utterance of my name.

Why have you hated me in your counsels?
For I shall be silent among those who are silent,
and I shall appear and speak.
Why then have you hated me, you Greeks?
Because I am a barbarian among (the) barbarians?
For I am (the wisdom) of the Greeks
and the knowledge of the barbarians.
I am the one whose image is great in Egypt

and the one who has no image among the barbarians.
I am the one who has been hated everywhere
and who has been loved everywhere.
I am the one whom they call Life,
and you have called Death.
I am the one whom they call Law,
and you have called Lawlessness.
I am the one whom you have pursued,
And I am the one you have seized.
I am the one whom you have scattered,
And you have gathered me together.

Bibliography

Amundsen, Christian, *Illumination: A Gnostic Handbook for the Post Modern World*, 1998.

Armstrong, Karen, *A History of God*, 1993.

Baring, Anne and Cashford, Jules, *The Myth of the Goddess*, 1991.

Barrie, Mary W., *Gnosticism*, 1926.

Bloom, Harold and Rosenberg, David, *The Book of J*, 1991.

Bruce, F.F., *Jesus and Christian Origins Outside the New Testament*, 1974.

Butler, E.M., *The Myth of the Magus*, 1948.

Catholic Encyclopedia.

Campbell Joseph, The Portable Jung, ed. R.F.C. Hull, Middlesex: Penguin Books, 1976.

Clifton, C.S., *Encyclopedia of Heresies and Heretics*, 1992.

Couliano, Ioan, *The Tree of Gnosis: Gnostic Mythology from Early Christianity to Modern Nihilism*, 1995.

Eliade, Mircea (ed.), *The Encyclopedia of Religion*, Macmillan, 1987.

Ellwood, Robert S. and Partin, Harry B, *Religious and Spiritual Groups in Modern America*, 1988.

Encyclopedia Britannica, 2001.

Ferguson and Wright, *New Dictionary of Theology*, 1988.

Filoramo, G., *A History of Gnosticism*, 1991.

Foerster, Werner, *Gnosis*, 1972.

Godwin, Joscelyn, *Mystery Religions of the Ancient World*, 1981.

Grant, Robert M. (ed.), *Gnosticism: An Anthology*, 1961.

Hedrick, Charles W. and Robert Hodgson Jnr (eds), *Nag Hammadi, Gnosticism & Early Christianity,* 1986.

Hastings, *Encyclopedia of Religion and Ethics.*

Henry, Patrick, *New Directions*, 1972.

Hexham, I., *Concise Dictionary of Religion*, 1993.

Hoeller, Stephen A., *Gnosticism: New Light on the Ancient Tradition of Inner Knowing.*

Holroyd, Stuart,*The Elements of Gnosticism*, 1994.

Hopkins, Keith, *A World Full of Gods*, 1999

Hornblower S. and Spamforth A. (eds), *Oxford Companion to Classical Civilisation*, 1998

Jonas, Hans, *Gnosticism and Modern Nihilism*, 1952.

Jonas, Hans, *The Gnostic Religion*, 1958.

Jung, Carl, *The Spiritual Problem of Modern Man*, 1933.

Jung, Carl, *Answer to Job*, 1954.

Key, H.C., Myers, E.M., Rogerson, J. and Saldarini, A.J., *Cambridge Companion to the Bible*, 1997.

King, C.W., *The Gnostics and Their Remains Ancient and Medieval*, 1864.

King, Francis, *Encyclopedia of Mind, Magic and Mythology Stories.*

King, Karen, *Images of the Feminine in Gnosticism*, ed. Studies in Antiquity & Christianity, 1988, Harrisburg, PA: Trinity Press International, 2000.

King, Karen, 'Mackinations on Myth and Origin' *in Reimagining Christian Origin*, 1996.

Latourette, Kenneth Scott, *A History of the expansion of Christianity*, vol. 1, Eyre and Spottiswoode, London.

Lebreton, J., *Gnosticism, Marcionism and Manicheism.*

Logan, Alastair H.B., *Gnosticism and Christian Heresy*, 1996.

Mather, H.A. and Nichols, L.A., *Dictionary of Cults, Sects, Religions and the Occult*, 1993.

McGrath, Alister, *Christian Theology – an Introduction*.

McManners, John (ed.), *The Oxford Illustrated History of Christianity*, 1990.

Mead, G.S.R., *Fragments of a Faith Forgotten*, 1900.

Mead, G.S.R., *Pistis Sophia*, 1921.

Mead, G.S.R., *Simon Magus*, 1892.

Mead, G.S.R., *Thrice Greatest Hermes: Studies in Hellenistic Theosophy and Gnosis*.

Murray, Gilbert, *Five Stages of Greek Religion*, The Thinkers Library No. 52, 1943.

Myer, Marvin (trans.), *The Gospel of Thomas: Hidden Sayings of Jesus*, 1992.

Pagels, Elaine, *Beyond Belief: the Secret Gospel of Thomas*, 2000.

Pagels, Elaine, *The Gnostic Gospels*, Vintage Publishers, 1980.

Poncé, Charles, *Kabbalah. An Introduction and Illumination for the World Today*, 1974.

Robinson, James M, *The Nag Hammadi Library*, 1990

Rudolf, Kurt, *Gnosis: The Nature and History of Gnosticism*, 1987.

Russell, Bertrand, *A History of Western Philosophy*, 1947.

Satinover, Jeffrey Burke, *Jungians and Gnostics*, 1994.

Smoley, Richard and Kinney, Jay, *Hidden Wisdom*.

Speer, Robert, *The Finality of Jesus Christ*.

Spong, J.S., *Christian Century*, 1979.

Williams, Michael Allen, *Rethinking 'Gnosticism': An Argument for Dismantling a Dubious Category*, 1999.

Wilson, R., *The Gnostic Problem – a Study of the Relations between Hellenistic Judaism and the Gnostic Heresy*, 1958.

Voegelin, Eric, The New Science of Politics, 1952.

Yamauchi, Edwin M., *Pre-Gnosticism*, 1973.

Further Reading

Bloom, Harold, *American Religion* (1992) and *Omens of Millennium* (1996), Fourth Estate.

Cooper, Rabbi David A., *God is a Verb, Kabbalah and the practice of mystical Judaism*, 1997 (ISBN1 5777777322 694).

Freke, Timothy and Gandy, Peter, *The Hermetica The Lost Wisdom of the Pharaohs*, Piatkus 1998

Freud, Sigmund, *Moses and Monotheism*, 1937.

Knight, C. and Lomas, R., *The Hiram Key*, 1997 (ISBN 0 09 969941 9).

Matthews, Caitlin, *Sophia Goddess of Wisdom* (ISBN 0 04 440590 1).

Pagels, Elaine, *Adam, Eve, and the Serpent* (1988), Weidenfeld and Nicolson.

Singer, June, *A Gnostic Book of Hours: Keys to Inner Wisdom*.

Websites

Boehme, Jacob. http://www.mythosandlogos.com/boehme.html.

Borce, Gjorgjevski. Gnosticism: Origins, Beliefs and Modern Tendencies. http://members.tripod.com/~aos/general/gnostic.html.

Davies, Vicki. Gnosticism. http://www.sd.com.au/db/gnostic.html.

Edwards, Dean. The Gnosis Archive. 1994. http://www.webcom.com/gnosis/overview.html

Gnostic Pagan Tradition. http://www.gnostics.com.

Gospel of Thomas. http://home.epix.net/~miser17/Thomas.html. (provides a list of best available books on the subject)

Hoeller, Stephen A. The Gnostic World View: A Brief Summary of Gnosticism. http://www.gnosis.org/gnintro.htm.

Hoeller, Stephen A. On the Trail of the Winged God. Hermes and Hermeticism Throughout the Ages. http://www.gnosis.org/hermes.html

Irenaeus of Lyons c.115 – c.202. http://www.earlychurch.org.uk/irenaeus.html0.

Mann, Judith. Legend of the Cathars. http://gnosistraditions.faithweb.com/mont.html.

McGee, M.D. Christianity Revealed – The Gnostics I. http://www.askwhy.co.uk/christianity/0760Gnostics.html

Non-Christian Gnosticism. http://home.sol.no/~noetic/prechr.html. (provides a short discussion about the Hermetics, Zoroastrians, Mandaeans, Simon Magus and the Peratae)

Owens, Lance S.: Introduction to Gnosticism and the Nag Hammadi Library. http://www.gnosis.org/naghamm/nhlintro.html.

Notes for Scholars

(1) The following items in The Gnostic Library predate Nag Hammadi:

Texts from the Askew Codex: The Pistis Sophia: Books of the Saviour. Also an introduction to Pistis Sophia by G.R.S. Mead. The Codex was bought by the British Museum in 1795. Where Dr Askew got it from is unknown.

Texts from the Bruce Codex: The Books of JEU and an Untitled Text. This Codex of Coptic, Arabic and Ethiopian manuscripts was found in Upper Egypt by Scottish traveller James Bruce in about 1769. The first translations began in mid-1800s. The Library's texts were translated by Carl Schmidt in 1892.

Texts from the Papyrus Berolinensis 8502 (Akhmin Codex): Gospel According to Mary, Apocryphon of John, Sophia of Jesus Christ. The Akhmin Codex is a fragment of a Coptic codex acquired in Cairo in 1896 by Dr Rheinhardt. By the time it was published in 1955, the Nag Hammadi texts had appeared with their version of the Apocryphon of John and the Sophia of Jesus Christ.

Gospel of Thomas fragments in the Papyrus Oxyrhyncus: fragments from the original Greek version discovered in 1897 and 1903 at Oxyrhyncus in Egypt, compared with a Coptic version of the complete and well preserved gospel found at Nag Hammadi.

Marcion and his writings: includes the Gospel of the Lord and other texts.

Gnostic Acts and other Classical Texts: The Hymn of Jesus and Mystery of the Cross from the Acts of John translated by G.R.S. Mead; The Acts of John and The Acts of Thomas with commentaries by M.R. James; Hymn of the Pearl from the Acts of Thomas; Odes of Solomon; The Secret Gospel of Mark. The Secret Gospel of Mark was discovered by Prof. Morton Smith in 1958. Along with all the other texts mentioned here it survived the early 'burning of the books'.

Gnostic Fragments in Patristic Sources: Translation of the Naassene Psalm quoted by Hippolytus in Refutations; Basilides fragments from works by Hippolytus, Clement of Alexandria, Origen; Ptolemy's Commentary on the Gospel of John Prologue found in Irenaeus Against Heresies, and Letter to Flora in Epiphanius's Against Heresies; Epiphanes On Righteousness found in Clement of Alexandria's Stromatics; Theodotus's The Excerpts Ex Theodoto also found in Clement of Alexandria's Stromatics; Heracleon – Fragments from his Commentary on the Gospel of John found in Origen's Commentary on the Gospel of John; the Ophite Diagrams, Celsus' and Origen's descriptions of one of them.

(2) The following items are included in the Nag Hammadi Library:

Writings of creative and redemptive mythology, including Gnostic alternative versions of creation and salvation: The Apocryphon of John, The Hypostasis of the Archons, On the Origin of the World, The Apocalypse of Adam, The Paraphrase of Shem.

Observations and commentaries on diverse Gnostic themes, such as the nature of reality, the nature of the soul, the relationship of the soul to the world: The Gospel of Truth, The Treatise on the Resurrection, The Tripartite Tractate, Eugnostos the Blessed, The

Second Treatise of the Great Seth, The Teachings of Silvanus, The Testimony of Truth.

Liturgical and Initiatory Texts: The Discourse on the Eighth and Ninth, The Prayer of Thanksgiving, A Valentinian Exposition, The Three Steles of Seth, The Prayer of the Apostle Paul.

Writings dealing primarily with the feminine deific and spiritual principle, particularly with the Divine Sophia: The Thunder, Perfect Mind, The Thought of Norea, The Sophia of Jesus Christ, the Exegesis of the Soul.

Writings pertaining to the lives and experiences of some of the apostles: The Apocalypse of Peter, The Letter of Peter to Philip, The Acts of Peter and the Twelve Apostles, The (First) Apocalypse of James, The (Second) Apocalypse of James, The Apocalypse of Paul.

Scriptures which contain sayings of Jesus as well as incidents in His life: The Dialogue of the Saviour, The Book of Thomas the Contender, The Apocryphon of James, The Gospel of Philip, The Gospel of Thomas.

Index

Index

Index

Index